A Love Song for the Sabbath

*How to experience
the joy that
God intended
when He gave us
the Sabbath.*

RICHARD M. DAVIDSON

Review and Herald Publishing Association
Washington, DC 20039-0555
Hagerstown, MD 21740

Printed in U.S.A.

Library of Congress Cataloging in Publication Data

Davidson, Richard M., 1946-
    A love song for the Sabbath/Richard M. Davidson.
        p.   cm.
    Includes bibliographies.
    ISBN 0-8280-0431-5

    1. Sabbath.   2. Seventh-day Adventists—Doctrines.
3. Adventists—Doctrines. I. Title.
BV125.D29 1988
263'.1—dc19   88-5105
                                                                       CIP·

DEDICATION

To Jo Ann,
Rahel and Jonathan—
sweet singers of the Sabbath song

Contents

ACKNOWLEDGMENTS

I owe an immense debt of gratitude to a host of individuals who have contributed to my love and appreciation for the Sabbath and have assisted in the preparation of this book.

Particular thanks go to my parents, who provided a Sabbath atmosphere of exquisite delight in our home as I was growing up. Numerous individuals have helped to shape my understanding of the meaning of the Sabbath, many of whom are listed in the footnotes of this book. Special credit goes to two beloved teachers who have recently passed to their rest: Dr. Richard Nies and Dr. Carsten Johnsen, although not directly cited in this work, have had a profound influence upon my thinking through their penetrating lectures on the subject.

I also wish to express specific appreciation to colleagues who have read and critiqued the manuscript; Selene Peck and Sharon Benson for carefully entering the material into the computer; and to Gerald Wheeler for his valuable editorial suggestions.

Most of all, I am grateful to my beloved wife and two precious children, from whom I have learned much about Sabbath joy, and to whom this book is dedicated. My ultimate thanks, of course, goes to God, for His marvelous gift of the Sabbath.

Introduction

While attending college, I met a sparkling young lady who worked in the school cafeteria. Every time I saw her she bubbled with enthusiasm and joy. I observed her character qualities, her winning ways, and through association with her both in and out of the cafeteria, I couldn't help myself—I fell in love!

And then my heart broke forth into song. Instead of poring over Greek vocabulary every spare minute, I found myself learning words to love songs and planning special occasions to sing to my beloved. Life turned into a symphony of celebration, and I must add, the more I have gotten to know my beloved (now my wife), the more joyous life has become. Being with Jo Ann has increasingly called forth a melody in my heart in celebration of our love.

When we got married, our wedding anniversaries seemed much too far apart, so we invented "monthaversaries." Birthdays were not enough, so we celebrated "unbirthdays." We celebrated, not because we had to, but because we wanted to. Thus we looked for every opportunity to do so. Hearts that sing with love can do nothing else.

God longs to celebrate with us a love relationship more intimate than anything human lovers have ever experienced. He loves us so much that He can't wait a whole year or even a month for special time with us. So every week He has set aside a whole day, a Sabbath, for intimate fellowship—an all-day date with us, His beloved.

In this book you will not find an exhaustive, systematic treatise proving that the seventh-day Sabbath is God's divinely appointed time for celebration. I will recount some of the abundant evidence that the seventh day is still God's Sabbath for Christians today. But this book deals primarily with what is to me the strongest kind of proof for the significance of the Sabbath. According to the old adage, "the proof of the pudding is in the eating." The Sabbath is not primarily a fact to prove, but a meaning to be discovered, a personal relationship to experience. Have you tasted its joy, sung its melody of life and peace?

Have you fallen in love with the Lord of the Sabbath? Has the Sabbath become to you a day of joy? Do you have a love song to sing to your beloved God on the Sabbath? Most of us are not very accomplished at writing our own love songs. We depend upon others who have also been enraptured with love. God knew our poetic limitations, so He Himself inspired a love song for the occasion of the Sabbath. His special love song, often ignored or neglected in studies of the Sabbath, lies tucked away in the heart of the Bible. If you desire to fall more deeply in love with your Lord, if you long to taste and see the joy of His Sabbath— this song is for you! Or if you are already experiencing an intimate fellowship with the Lord on the Sabbath and are searching for an appropriate way to express your senti- ments of love—this song will fulfill your quest.

The Bible's love song for the Sabbath is the ninety- second psalm. It has the superscription, or heading, "A psalm. A song. For the Sabbath day." In the following chapters we shall see how the sublime poetry of Psalm 92 embodies the biblical mood and meaning of the Sabbath. The psalm is indeed a love song: the singers exclaim to the Lord, "It is good . . . to proclaim your love in the morning and your faithfulness at night" (verses 1, 2). Although the original tune to these divinely-inspired lyrics has vanished, the Hebrew poetry and the rhymed English paraphrases of Psalm 92 have been set to music (see Appendix). However, we may best recapture the spirit of the original melody as this psalm becomes a song of experience in our lives. Come, let us sing a new song—the love Song for the Sabbath!

Chapter I

"Psalm 92—A Love Song for the Sabbath"

Before we begin to "sing" the 92nd psalm, let us first pause to consider some of the intriguing features of this psalm which underscore its unique status as the Sabbath Love Song of the Bible.

Psalm 92 is the only psalm in the book of Psalms expressly connected with the Sabbath. Its title, or superscription, reads: "A psalm. A song. For the Sabbath day." Some scholars have tended to discount the heading as a later addition unrelated to the psalm's original setting or purpose. However, we find no manuscript evidence to support such skepticism. All of the earliest Hebrew manuscripts (e.g., the Dead Sea scrolls) and other ancient versions (e.g., the Greek Septuagint) contain the superscription. In New Testament times God's people accepted the headings of the Psalms as authentic. For example, Jesus Himself based His final clinching argument for His Messiahship upon the validity and reliability of the superscriptions in the Psalms.[1] If we take the text of Scripture seriously in its present canonical form, we must conclude that Psalm 92 is a psalm, or song, intimately related to the Sabbath day.

Numerous literary features of the psalm highlight the number seven, thus providing internal evidence that the author intended to connect it with the Sabbath. Only in the Sabbath psalm (among the 150 psalms in the psalter) do we find the divine name Yahweh, or Lord, repeated seven times.[2] The psalm contains seven different epithets for the wicked and seven positive qualities of the righteous.[3] Again, the mid-point and climax of the psalm (vs. 8) is flanked by seven verses (1-7 and 9-15) on either side.[4] Furthermore, the overall structure of the psalm contains five stanzas (or strophes), each with six lines, except for the climactic middle stanza, which contains seven lines. As F. Delitzsch puts it: "Certainly the unmistakable strophe-schema too, 6.6.7.6.6., is not without significance. The middle of the psalm bears the stamp of the sabbatic number." [5]

The inspired author of this intricately wrought psalm employs a common literary device in Scripture that reveals the poem's unity and central thrust, and further under-scores its "sevenness." Scholars call this device a "chiasm," [6] but as an inveterate backpacker, I like to call it "a mountain-climbing structure." Just as in climbing a mountain one encounters specific types of plants and animals living together in a certain order in what scientists call ecological zones, and then upon descending the other side of the mountain, the zones appear in reverse order; so in a literary chiasm we find a reverse parallelism: the first item parallels what comes last; the second item parallels what appears next to last, the third parallels the third from last, etc. Also, just as when climbing a mountain, the climax of the experience is the view from the top of the mountain, so in biblical chiasms the central and most important point usually appears at the center, or midpoint, of the literary work.

Psalm 92 is an elegantly designed chiasm, or "mountain-climbing" structure:

We will take up the details of our chiastic (or mountain-climbing) structure in later chapters, as we see how the psalm unfolds the rich meaning of the Sabbath and high-lights the central issue in Sabbath observance. But for now we will just note that the poem divides into seven different thematic/structural sections, which climax in the central statement of verse 8. Again we see the strong sevenness of the poem.

THE CHIASTIC STRUCTURE OF PSALM 92

EXALTATION
(God's Character)

D

vs 8
(1 line)

REDEMPTION C
(God's work in the past)

C[1] REDEMPTION
(God's work in the future)

vs 7   vs 9
(3 lines)   (3 lines)

CREATION B
(God's creative works)

vss 4-6   vss 10-12
(6 lines)   (6 lines)

B[1] SANCTIFICATION
(God's re-creative work)

A
EXULTATION
(God's character)

vss 1-3   vss 13-15
(6 lines)   (6 lines)

A[1]
GLORIFICATION
(God's character)

This pattern of sevens running throughout the psalm, coupled with the explicit mention of the purpose of the psalm in the title—"for the Sabbath"—seems to underscore its clear relationship to the Sabbath. Postexilic Judaism recognized the relationship by singing this psalm every Sabbath morning at the time of the drink offering and on the offering of the first lamb.[7] Today Jews still chant the psalm in the synagogue as part of the Sabbath morning service. Ellen White also points to a close tie between Psalm 92 and the Sabbath.[8]

If Psalm 92 is a psalm "for the Sabbath," then certainly it has a special message for Sabbath worshipers. The Jewish Talmud recognizes the sabbatical character of the psalm,[9] and recently a modern Jewish scholar has argued that the contents of this psalm correspond to and describe major themes of the biblical Sabbath.[10] Personal study of this

A LOVE SONG FOR THE SABBATH

magnificent song and other biblical material on the Sabbath has led me to conclude that Psalm 92 encompasses the prevailing mood and essential meaning of the biblical Sabbath. Therefore our outline for the remainder of this book will follow the stanzas of God's love song for the Sabbath. Let's now sing the first stanza of Hymn (Psalm) 92!

References

[1] See Matthew 22:41-46. Jesus' whole argument rests on an acceptance of the authenticity of the superscription to Psalm 110, which indicates Davidic authorship.

[2] Franz Delitzsch, *Psalms*, vol. 5, C. F. Keil and F. Delitzsch, eds., *Commentary on the Old Testament:* (Grand Rapids: William B. Eerdmans, n.d.), book 3, pp. 66, 67; Nahum M. Sarna, "The Psalm for the Sabbath Day [Ps. 92]," *Journal of Biblical Literature* 81 (1962): 167, 168; Jacob Bazak, "Geometric Structural Patterns in Biblical Hebrew Poetry" (paper presented at the annual meeting of the Society of Biblical Literature, Anaheim, California, 1985).

[3] Bazak.

[4] *Ibid.*

[5] Delitzsch, p. 67.

[6] For a detailed discussion of literary chiastic structures, see John Welch, ed., *Chiasmus in Antiquity* (Hildersheim: Gerstenberg Verlag, 1981).

[7] See *The SDA Bible Commentary* (Washington, D.C.: Review and Herald Pub. Assn., 1978), Vol. 3, p. 845; Delitzsch, p. 66; cf. B. Rosh Ha-Shana 31a.

[8] Ellen G. White, *The Desire of Ages* (Mountain View, Calif.: Pacific Press Pub. Assn., 1940), pp. 281, 282.

[9] See Delitzsch, p. 66.

[10] Sarna, pp. 158-168.

Chapter 2

A Song of Exultation

It is good to praise the Lord
and make music to your name, O Most High,

to proclaim your love in the morning
and your faithfulness at night,

to the music of the ten-stringed lyre
and the melody of the harp.
—Ps. 92:1-3

The opening stanza of the Bible's love song for the Sabbath sets the tone for the remainder of the psalm. Joy overflows in every line. The Sabbath is no day of gloom, but a time of exultation! God's people praise and sing (verse 1). The worshipers simply must declare the love and faithfulness of the Lord (verse 2). It is an occasion for instrumental music—a time of exuberant celebration.

Unfortunately, for many the Sabbath has not been a day of delight. Like some of the rabbis in Jesus' time, they have bound up its hours with a multitude of negative restrictions and wearisome regulations, until the Sabbath has become an almost unbearable burden. For many young people the Sabbath has become one big "Thou shalt not." The only good thing about the day is that it does eventually come to an end. Many, as in Nehemiah's time, can't wait until Sabbath sunset so they can get on with their buying and selling. Sabbath is an interruption to their lives, an intrusion upon their schedules—in short, an unwelcome guest. But that is not God's plan for the Sabbath!

A Day of Exquisite Delight

God longs for the Sabbath to be the "most joyful day of the week," a "delight, the day of days."[1] To each one of us He extends the invitation: "The Sabbath—oh!—make it the sweetest, the most blessed day of the whole week."[2]

Is this your experience on the Sabbath? Has the Sabbath become a song of love flowing spontaneously from a heart in love? The first verse of Psalm 92 emphasizes the Sabbath theme of love and joy. The first word of the psalm in Hebrew perhaps summarizes the essence of the day: it is *tov*, which not only means "good"; it denotes the quintessence of wholesomeness, pleasure, happiness, and beauty.[3]

In Isaiah 58:13, 14 we find the answering chord to the keynote of joy introduced in Psalm 92. God promises that "if you call the Sabbath a *delight [oneg]. . .* then you will find your *joy (anog)* in the Lord." The Old Testament uses many different words for joy, happiness, pleasure, and delight, each of which appears numerous times. But the Hebrew root (*ng*) behind this special word in Isaiah 58 (*oneg*) occurs as a noun only one other time, where it describes the palaces of royalty. As a verb it appears in the Bible only 10 times. This rich Hebrew word denotes not just that which brings delight, but in particular that which delights because of its surpassing quality, that which satisfies and pleases because it has a delicate beauty or regal charm. In short, "exquisite delight."[4]

Sabbath Delight in Ancient Israel

The faithful worshiper in ancient Israel caught the vision of the exquisite delight of the Sabbath. In order to heighten our sense of festal exultation, let us for a few moments join with Israel of old in savoring the exquisite delight of the Sabbath. Come, let's celebrate the Sabbath in old Jerusalem! Imagine that we either live in the vicinity of Jerusalem so we

A Song of Exultation

can go to the Temple on Sabbath, or that we are visiting from more distant parts of Palestine for a high Sabbath. It is the preparation day, the day before the Sabbath. Envision ourselves among the bands of happy pilgrims making their way along the roads and paths leading upward to Mount Zion. Of course, we sing the songs of Zion as we travel the dusty trails.

Some of us have journeyed from the west, and we reach the summit of the forested pass just beyond Kirjath-jearim. Others of us have come from the north, and have traveled from Shechem on the road that twists through the hilly country of olive groves and vineyards until it reaches the lookout over Jerusalem near Gibeon. Coming from the east, some of us have climbed up the desolate Jericho road through the wilderness of Judea and surmounted the heights of the Mount of Olives. Or from the south we passed through Bethlehem, round the bend, and past the tomb of Rachel.

Regardless from whichever direction we've journeyed, when we come into view of the holy city, we find ourselves hushed to silence by the sounds and sight of the Temple mount. A priest stands on the southwest cornerstone of the Temple enclosure, calling us to the Sabbath festival with blasts from the shofar (an ibex's or ram's horn). Can you picture the scene in your mind's eye?

Archaeologists have recently dug up the very stone where the priest stood in Christ's day, a giant ashlar block with the inscription still visible—"The place for the blowing of the shofar." Can you hear in your mind's ear the clarion tones of the shofar blasts? In Jesus' time six blasts announced the eve of the Sabbath:

> "The first, for people to cease work in the fields; the second, for the city and shops to cease work; the third, for the lights to be kindled. . . . Then there was an interval for as long as it takes to bake a small fish, or to put a loaf in the oven, and then a long blast, a series of short blasts, and a long blast were blown, and one commenced the Sabbath." [5]

A LOVE SONG FOR THE SABBATH

As we hear the call to celebrate the Sabbath feast, we break into singing and, with praise in our hearts, make our way to Mount Zion. What joy awaits us at the Temple worship! A description of the Temple music helps capture some of the joy of the occasion. If we piece together the biblical information,[6] a picture unfolds of three antiphonal choirs comprised of descendants of each of the sons of Levi. The Kohathites stood directly in front of the Temple steps that led from the court of Israel. The sons of Merari positioned themselves on the left, and the sons of Gershom took their places on the right. Can you hear them singing responsively, raising songs of joy, accompanied by harps and lyres, cymbals and high-pitched cymbals, and—can you imagine it—120 trumpets. What a majestic celebration! Now the words of Psalm 92 take on added meaning: "It is good to praise the Lord and make music to your name, O Most High, to proclaim your love in the morning and your faithfulness at night, to the music of the ten-stringed lyre and the melody of the harp" (Ps. 92:1-3).

Sabbath Joy in the Jewish Home

The home services during the Sabbath are no less joyful than those at the Temple. Though Scripture does not record the precise details of the special Friday evening service, Jewish sources reveal the broad contours of the celebration in Jesus' day,[7] and modern observant Jews have preserved many of the ancient customs.[8] Despite the many rabbinic regulations and prohibitions followed by modern Jewish celebrants, we find, nonetheless, a dominant theme of joy and delight—exquisite delight. Our imaginations may be stirred to recapture some of the joy of ancient Israelite households in welcoming the Sabbath as we visit a traditional Jewish home in Israel today at the eve of the approaching *Shabbat* ("Sabbath").

The mood is one of expectancy. The Shabbat is the day around which all the other days of the week revolve. We feel ourselves sheltered in the shadow of the past Shabbat until Tuesday, and from Wednesday on the family already basks

A Song of Exultation

in the light of the approaching Shabbat. The Shabbat is so special that Judaism has personified its qualities as those of a queen and a bride.[9]

Already on Wednesday the family members have begun preparations for the approach of royalty. Cakes and other confections—all kinds of special Sabbath delicacies—are prepared. On Friday the stores have all closed by noon. Father hurries home with the fresh braided challah bread and wine, and with the bouquet of Sabbath flowers from one of the numerous sidewalk stands. Everyone pitches in to clean the house; all have taken their baths, and everything is ready, not just in order to fulfill the commandment to cease work on Sabbath but to be ready to receive the royal guest, Queen Shabbat! The queen is coming at set of sun.

The table has a festive appearance. The mother has set it for the Sabbath meal and covered it with a white cloth. On it she has placed a special set of Sabbath dishes, two Sabbath loaves of challah bread, the bottle of wine (we would use grape juice), silver candlesticks and candles, and Sabbath flowers. The family members have dressed in their best clothes. All are ready to receive the royal guest.

Long before the sun actually sets, the family, in their eager expectation, begins their Sabbath celebration. The mother, as queen of the home, has the honor of officially receiving the Sabbath by kindling the Sabbath lights. The children watch with wonder as she lights at least two candles. Then we hear her offering a prayer of blessing upon the family:

O God of Your people Israel: You are holy and You have made the Sabbath and the people of Israel holy. You have called upon us to honor the Sabbath with light, with joy, and with peace—As a king and queen give love to one another; as a bride and her bridegroom—so have we kindled these two lights for love of Your daughter, the Sabbath day. God, grant me and all my loved ones a chance to truly rest on this

A LOVE SONG FOR THE SABBATH

Sabbath day. May the light of the candles drive out from among us the spirit of anger, the spirit of harm; send Your blessing to my children, that they may walk in the ways of Your Torah, Your light. May You ever be their God and mine, O Lord, my Creator and my Redeemer. Amen.

Then the father tenderly takes his children in his arms or places his hands on their bowed heads and recites a blessing for each. For the sons he says:

May God make you like unto Ephraim and Manasseh!

And for the daughters:

May God make you like Sarah, Rebekah, Rachel, and Leah!

Then for all comes the priestly dedication:

May the Lord bless you and keep you; may the Lord cause His countenance to shine upon you, and be gracious unto you; may the Lord lift up His countenance toward you and give you peace.

The woman's place of honor on the Sabbath and her exalted position in the home again receive emphasis. The husband sings to his wife from Proverbs 31, extolling her virtues:

A woman of valor who can find? For her price is far above rubies . . . Many women have done virtuously, but thou excellest them all!

Next comes the Sabbath meal. It begins with the sanctfication of the Sabbath over a cup of wine (symbolizing joy and cheer), the blessing over the challah bread, and the

A Song of Exultation

special Sabbath courses. On Sabbath the family eats the choicest food of all the week. Before each course someone says, "For the honor of the Sabbath!" During the meal the family heartily sings joyous table hymns reflecting the feeling and mood of the Sabbath. In the singing, eating, and fellowship the family can forget their weekday burdens, worries, and sorrows.

And so the Sabbath progresses. Friday evening is a time of family fellowship, of special intimacy between husband and wife. On Sabbath morning the central theme is revelation. As the congregation listens to the reading of the Torah in the synagogue, the mood is quiet and more intellectual. Then comes another meal with more table hymns and sumptuous dishes.

The evening meal carries the theme of redemption and Messiah, with the mood of yearning, longing, and beauty. The family members quote and discuss passages of Scripture around the table, and the blessed fellowship often lasts well into the evening. The special home service to usher out the Sabbath is called *Havdalah,* "separation [of holy time from the nonholy time of the rest of the week]" and includes blessings over candlelight, wine, and special fragrances from spices or flowers. No one hurries. Reluctant to let their special "guest" go for another week, the family often prolongs their celebration till long after the sun actually sets. They cherish the Sabbath's exquisite delight as transcending all earthly bliss.

Capturing the Joy

Such a sense of exquisite delight is what God longs for each of us to enjoy on the holy hours of the Sabbath. At the approach of the Sabbath we indeed welcome Royalty—the great King, the Almighty, comes to be with us—or better, invites us to be with Him—for 24 hours of celebration and fellowship. Does not this thought transform preparation for the Sabbath from a frenzy to keep a commandment to a joyous expectancy in awaiting the arrival of a royal Guest? Does not such a concept transform the observance of the

A LOVE SONG FOR THE SABBATH

Sabbath from a legalistic duty into an exquisite delight?

How well have we captured the joy of the Sabbath as God originally intended His people to experience it? Perhaps it would be well for us to adapt some of the delightful customs of our Jewish Sabbathkeeping brothers and sisters, many of whom reflect the practices of biblical times. Could we, for example, create a festive family candlelighting ceremony at the commencement and conclusion of the Sabbath? In Israel such services so overjoyed us that we bought a menorah (candelabra) so we could incorporate the custom into our Sabbath celebration. The eyes of our son and daughter sparkle as they watch the flickering Sabbath candles. Why not a festively decorated table, with candlelight and flowers? And why not unfermented Sabbath wine? Why not toast the joy of the Sabbath? Why not eat Sabbath bread? Until very recently our children did not use the word dessert—they chose the term Sabbath bread! Why not tie such culinary delicacies to the joy of the Sabbath? Could we initiate the singing of joyous Sabbath table songs throughout each meal? The new *SDA Hymnal* has included several appropriate traditional Jewish hymns (see Nos. 387, 395, and 674). Could we introduce a special Sabbath greeting? We say amen and hallelujah—two good Hebrew words. Perhaps we could add to our vocabulary *Shabbat shalom!* (Sabbath peace!), to greet each other on Sabbath, as our Jewish friends do.

Even our Sabbath vespers might seem more distinctly Sabbath-oriented if we changed the name from vespers (derived from high church liturgy) and substituted the phrase from Isaiah 58, as used in the synagogue, *Oneg Shabbat* (Joy of the Sabbath). And on and on we could go with countless other suggestions for Sabbath traditions found in Jewish customs.

The Difference It Makes

I can give personal testimony to the difference introducing such joyful Sabbath traditions has made in our home. It makes my heart sing to hear my little girl and boy often

A Song of Exultation

pray during the week, "Dear Jesus, please make it to be Sabbath again soon." The Sabbath joy and holiness, so precious in our home while we are celebrating it, seems to spill over into the other days, imbuing them also with an extra measure of exquisite delight.

Our family has found it true that "for those who hear the music of the Sabbath, the seventh day comes like a jubilee. Every week it is a gift of gladness, a holiday to cheer our waiting hearts."[10]

The Motivation for Sabbath Joy

Psalm 92:1-3 captures in poetry such music of the Sabbath. But the psalm also reminds us that traditions and customs in themselves are not enough, as beautiful and meaningful as they may be. Our celebration cannot be contrived or forced. Rather, it must flow forth spontaneously from a singing heart, a heart that has fallen in love, or all the beautiful traditions will deteriorate into meaningless forms. Thus the ninety-second psalm not only gives us the *mood* of Sabbath, one of joy and exquisite delight, but points us to the *motivation* for that joy, found in the deep *meaning* and *message* of the Sabbath.

Already in the first three verses of our psalm we have found hints of profound meaning. In verse one the psalmist sings praises to the Lord's name. Throughout Scripture the name of the Lord stands for His character (See Ex. 34:5-7). There the name used for God is "Lord," or *Yahweh*. In the next chapter we will see that it is God's covenant name, revealing the very qualities mentioned in verse 2 of our Sabbath psalm: His "love" and "faithfulness." The Hebrew word for "love," *chesed*, is no mere sentimental emotion, but steadfast covenant love, love that will not let me go. The word for "faithfulness," *emunah*, is literally "firmness, solidity," and is related to the word *amen*. The Lord has entered into a personal relationship with us, a marriage covenant, so to speak. And His vows of faithfulness and love are amen and amen! He will never let us go! Furthermore, He is not only a personal, loving God; according to the last part of verse 1, he is the "Most High," the transcendant, omnipotent God. He is all powerful and all loving. No wonder the psalmist broke forth into a Sabbath song of love, both in the morning and at night. Beholding the character of his God put a song in his heart!

How good it is to thank the Lord,
And praise to Thee, Most High, accord,
To show Thy love with morning light,
And tell Thy faithfulness each night;
Yea, good it is Thy praise to sing,
And all our sweetest music bring

(Ps. 92:1-3, paraphrased).

References

[1] Ellen G. White, *Testimonies for the Church* (Mountain View, Calif.: Pacific Press Pub. Assn., 1948), Vol. 6, p. 359.

[2] _____, *Child Guidance* (Nashville: Southern Pub. Assn., 1954), p. 532.

[3] See Andrew Boling, *"Tob,"* in R. Laird Harris et al., eds., *Theological Wordbook of the Old Testament* (Chicago: Moody Bible Institute, 1980), Vol. 1, pp. 345, 346.

[4] F. Brown, S. R. Driver, and C. A. Briggs, *A Hebrew and English Lexicon of the Old Testament* (Oxford: Clarendon Press, 1952), p. 772.

[5] Shab. 35b, cited by Robert M. Johnston, "The Rabbinic Sabbath," in Kenneth A. Strand, ed., *The Sabbath in Scripture and History* (Washington, D.C.: Review and Herald Pub. Assn., 1982), p. 85.

[6] See especially 1 Chron. 6, 16; 2 Chron. 5; Ezra 3; and Ps. 150.

[7] See the summary in Johnston, pp. 83-87.

[8] See Abraham E. Millgram, *Sabbath: The Day of Delight* (Philadelphia: The Jewish Publication Society of America, 1944).

[9] See especially the discussion in Abraham Heschel, *The Sabbath* (New York: Harper and Row, 1951), pp. 54, 65, 126-128.

[10] Charles Scriven, *Jublilee of the World* (Nashville: Southern Pub. Assn., 1978), p. 15.

Chapter 3

A Song of Creation

For you make me glad by your deeds, O Lord;
I sing for joy at the works of your hands.
How great are your works, O Lord,
how profound your thoughts!
The senseless man does not know,
fools do not understand.
—Ps. 92:4-6

Why does the psalmist exult so in his Sabbath song? He sings, "For [or because] you have made me glad *by your deeds, O Lord;* I sing for joy at the *works of your hands.*"

The Sabbath reminds the psalmist of Creation, and as he looks upon the works of the Creator's hands, he spontaneously sings for joy. The Hebrew expression for "your deeds," usually appears in connection with God's mighty acts throughout history (see Ps. 44:1; 64:9; 90:16; 111:3; 143:5), and the phrase "the works of your hands" most often has reference to God's activity in Creation (see Ps. 8:3, 6; 19:1). Though the psalmist cites both God's creative and redemptive work as grounds for Sabbath joy, he takes the latter up more fully in the next stanza, while the repetition of "works" in verse 5 seems to focus the theme of the present stanza upon God as the Creator.

A LOVE SONG FOR THE SABBATH

Creation and Joy

Our Sabbath song of Creation in Psalm 92 is nothing less than an echo from the time of Creation and from the realm of celestial glory. From out of the whirlwind the Lord Himself told Job that at the time of the earth's creation, "the morning stars sang together and all the angels shouted for joy" (Job 38:7).

What is it about Creation that calls forth such songs of joy? Let's go back to the origin of our earth, recorded in the opening pages of Scripture, to watch the drama of Creation unfold.

With divine fiat God could have instantaneously called a perfect completed world into existence. But rather, with the heavenly intelligences watching, He presents an awesome drama before the whole universe. According to Genesis 1, God's work represents nothing less than a *divine poem* written in the structure of space. Just as God often *speaks* in poetry in Scripture, so in the beginning He *creates* in poetic beauty. Genesis 1:1, 2 gives the introduction to the poem: "In the beginning God created the heavens and the earth." The introduction portrays the created earth as at first "without form" and "void," or literally, "unformed" and "unfilled." Dramatically and aesthetically, God proceeds to form and fill the heavens and the earth. The basic characteristic of ancient poetry is parallelism, or thought rhyme, in which the author places one line in parallel with a succeeding line that completes the thought (or action) of the previous line. So on the first three days of Creation the Master Poet forms the unformed, on the canvas of space, and on the succeeding three days He fills that which He has formed.

On the first day He calls forth the light, then on the matching fourth day He fills that light to completion with the sun and moon. During the second day God forms the sea and sky, and on the corresponding fifth day He fills the seas with fish and the sky with birds. The third day He makes the dry land appear and covers it with vegetation, and on the paralleling sixth day He once more fills what He

A Song of Creation

has formed, and the land animals and man walk on the earth and eat the plants. We may diagram God's divine poem in space as follows:

Introduction

1. Light
2. Sea and sky
3. Land and vegetation

4. Sun and moon
5. Fish in sea, birds in sky
6. Land animals (man), who eat vegetation

For six evenings and mornings the divine poem unfolds. But the Lord does not complete His creation on the sixth day. According to the most accurate translation of Genesis 2:2, "On *the seventh day* God finished His work that He had done." What is His finishing touch on the divine poem of Creation? As the sun sets on the sixth day, God has an extraordinary surprise for the newly created world and its inhabitants. He doesn't construct an elaborate shrine in some location as a memorial of His created work. That would give those worshipers living closer an advantage over those dwelling farther away. For the royal pair who are to rule in Eden (see Genesis 1:28) He doesn't build a spacious palace that soon could not contain the increasing population. Rather, God chooses to erect an everlasting edifice available to all humanity— a "palace" in time.[1] And He calls that special palace *Shabbat*, the Sabbath.

Creation and Celebration

Note with what meticulous and loving care He erects His glorious palace. Genesis 2:3, 4 describes the three distinct steps God takes. First, "on the seventh day He *rested* from all His work." Here the Hebrew verb for "rest" is *shābat*, from the same root as the noun *Shabbat*, or Sabbath. It means literally to "cease [working], pause, rest."[2] God ceased from His work, He paused and rested, not because He was physically tired — He is the one who "does not grow faint or grow weary" (Isa. 40:28, RSV). Rather, God, as the

A LOVE SONG FOR THE SABBATH

Great Exemplar, was preparing in time a palace of rest for humanity, whom He made in His own image. As the fourth commandment (Ex. 20:11) makes explicit, God's rest was to serve as a model for our own. Exodus 20 further enriches the meaning of God's rest by employing another term—*nuach*—which connotes not only cessation from toil but "tranquility, serenity, peace, and repose."[3] Such a rest God gives as a gift to the human race.

To highlight the quality of divine rest on that first Sabbath, the description in Exodus 31:17 adds another word for rest: "On the seventh day he abstained from work and rested [*nāphash*]" — literally, "took on new life, breathed freely, was refreshed."[4] Can you visualize God breathing a deep sigh of contentment as He contemplates His finished work? "Ahh!" Can you imagine Him "rejoicing in his whole world and delighting in mankind" (Prov. 8:31)? God ceases His work and pauses to enter into restful and refreshing fellowship with the man and woman He has made. He invites humanity to partake of this same rest.

The gift of rest. We see how such a gift is all the more extraordinary when we examine the Creation stories of other nations in the ancient Near East. There only the gods have opportunity to rest. In the Babylonian account, for example, the victorious gods create mankind from the blood of the dead god Kingu. As a "lowly, primitive creature," man exists to save the lesser gods from menial labor. Men are created to become slaves so that "the gods may then have rest."[5] In contrast to such a picture, God *shares* His rest with the man and woman who are not His slaves but His friends!

As a second step in God's preparation of the palace in time, "God *blessed* the seventh day" (Gen. 2:3). Earlier in the Creation week God had blessed the birds, fish, and man and woman. In Scripture, when God blesses, He imbues that which is blessed with power of fruitfulness and vitality to fulfill the function for which He intended it.[6] What a gift God bestows with His blessing upon the seventh day! A day

A Song of Creation

full of power designed to revitalize—to exhilarate—those who participate in its blessing.

As if divine rest and blessing were not enough, God completes the palace by His gift of holiness: "And God blessed the seventh day and *made it holy*" (verse 3). Here the Hebrew verb *ādash* is variously translated as "hallowed" (RSV), "sanctified" (NASB, KJV), "declared it holy" (TLB), and "made it holy" (NEB, NAB, NIV). The basic idea behind the verb is to separate, or set it apart, for a special use.[7] From the time of Creation, God sets apart the seventh day as special holy time. Thus the holiness of the seventh-day Sabbath does not depend upon whether or not man honors it, but is instead rooted in an act of God. As Abraham Heschel puts it: "Even when men forsake the Sabbath, its holiness remains."[8]

For what special purpose did God set the Sabbath apart? In what does its holiness consist? From the account of Moses at the burning bush (Ex. 3:1-6), the erection of the tabernacle (Ex. 25:8; 29:43), and other examples from Scripture,[9] we learn that it is *God's presence* that confers holiness.

The Sabbath is holy because God fills it with His presence. Therefore the Sabbath is not just a day; but a Person! In a special way during its hours God gives not only rest and power but, most important, Himself. On Sabbath He comes to tabernacle with us in person. It is the day of days for intimate fellowship and celebration with our Creator and Friend. As we contemplate what God has set aside for man, how can we help exclaiming: "The Sabbath is the most precious present mankind has received from the treasure house of God"?[10] It is so because the gift contains the Giver!

Now we can begin to understand why Scripture does not mention any explicit command in the beginning for humanity to observe the Sabbath. Genesis 1 and 2 contain no statement by God requiring that every seventh day man shall celebrate the Sabbath. With His divine law of love in man's heart, God did not need to *command* His created beings to celebrate the Sabbath. When my wife, Jo Ann, and I fell in love and got married, I did not say to her after the first year of marriage, "Next week is our anniversary, and if you don't celebrate with me there will be big trouble." When my daughter's birthday approaches I don't tell her, "You'd better celebrate that birthday or else." As I write these lines her eighth birthday is almost three months away, yet she is already counting the days on the calendar. I don't have to command her to celebrate—she wouldn't miss it for the world.

In the same way, when God set up the Sabbath—the "birthday of the world,"[11] a day of celebration—and when Adam and Eve understood the intimate fellowship He longed to have with them each week, it would have been completely out of character for Him to say, "Now you'd better celebrate." The great and loving God was offering to come and fellowship with them in person one whole day each week. Who would want to miss it? It was Adam and Eve's greatest delight. After having celebrated that first wonderful Sabbath with God, can't you hear them talking with each other as the next Sabbath approaches? "On the weekdays we have been able to see God for a little while when He walks with us in the cool of day, but Sabbath is coming! He'll be here to spend all day with us." I'm sure they could hardly wait, counting off the hours till Sabbath would arrive. When their hearts were in tune and in love with their Creator, it was their most natural and spontaneous desire to spend that day with Him.

Creation and the Creator

For Adam and Eve the Sabbath was a treasured time to fall more deeply in love with the Creator God, to gain new admiration for His character. The account of Creation scintillates with beauty, drama, and majesty, but even more exciting than the facts of Creation is the picture of God that shines forth from the opening chapters of Genesis. Chapters 1 and 2 contain two complimentary Creation accounts emphasizing different aspects of His character. Genesis 1

A Song of Creation

calls the Creator "God"—*Elohim*. It is the generic name for God, meaning the Almighty, the transcendent One, who stands above His creation, who speaks and it is done. He is the universal, cosmic Being, the infinite God. The second Creation account of Genesis 2 adds another name, referring to the Creator as "the Lord," *Yahweh*, His personal covenant name. He is the one who comes down to be with His creatures, to enter into an intimate, loving relationship with them.

James Weldon Johnson vividly captures this twofold picture of God's character in the closing lines of his poem "The Creation": [12]

> Up from the bed of the river
> God scooped the clay;
> And by the bank of the river
> He kneeled Him down:
> And there the great God Almighty
> Who lit the sun and fixed it in the sky,
> Who flung the stars to the most far corner of the night,
> Who rounded the earth in the middle of His hand;
> This Great God,
> Like a mammy bending over her baby,
> Kneeled down in the dust
> Toiling over a lump of clay
> Till He shaped it in His own image;
>
> Then into it He blew the breath of life,
> And man became a living soul.
> Amen. Amen.

Only the biblical God is both Elohim and Yahweh, both infinite and personal. The gods of the East are infinite— pantheistic—but impersonal. The gods of the West, the Greek pantheon, were most personal—quarreling, killing and being killed—but they were not infinite. Only the Judeo-Christian God can meet man's twofold need of an infinite reference point and a personal relationship.

A LOVE SONG FOR THE SABBATH

A beautiful picture of our Creator God emerges from Genesis, but Scripture contains a third story of Creation, one often overlooked, that gives us an even more intimate glimpse into the character of God and His relationship to His creation. Proverbs 8 portrays as personified wisdom one whom many commentators see as Jesus Himself. The chapter is especially intriguing because it not only describes what happened at Creation but reveals what went on in the mind of God, what He was thinking about as He created. Note in particular verses 29-31, the words of Wisdom (the Son):

When he gave the sea its boundary
     so the waters would not overstep his command,
and when he marked out the foundations of the earth.
     Then I was the craftsman at his side.
I was filled with delight day after day,
     rejoicing [literally, "sporting, playing,
laughing"] always in his presence,
     rejoicing in his whole world and delighting in
mankind.

What was God's own experience while He created? Was it not a grand celebration? Did the Godhead not rejoice in Their work, the Father, the Son (see John 1:1-3)—and the Holy Spirit (see Genesis 1:2)—working together and in great joy fellowshipping with one another, delighting in the things They had made, and as a climax, delighting in humanity?

Proverbs 9 completes the story with beautiful imagery. In verse 1, Divine Wisdom "has built her house; she has hewn out its seven pillars." The house of Creation is done, the seven pillars (perhaps representing the week) have been put into place, and in verses 2-6 Wisdom invites man to come and feast, to have table fellowship, to celebrate with God. The Creator God—He is all-powerful, (Gen. 1), all-loving (Gen. 2), and all-joyful (Prov. 8). What a God!

A Song of Creation

Creation, Law and Grace

Open communion, personal and intimate fellowship with such a wonderful God—such was the privilege of Adam and Eve to enjoy in their all-day Sabbath dates with Him. They wouldn't have missed them for anything. Sabbath-keeping was not a point designed to prove loyalty in Eden, for it was Adam and Eve's fondest expectation and delight to meet with their Creator each Sabbath.

But Paradise *did* have a test: the forbidden tree of knowledge of good and evil. A small, painless test that would allow Adam and Eve to taste the joy of obedience in a matter of ultimate morality—where His bidding was the *only* reason to obey. In the next chapter we will study why it was necessary and how they failed.

After the Fall, the curse of sin turned human nature inward in selfishness, instead of outward toward God. With his bent toward self, man no longer had a natural desire to fellowship with God. Sin brought the broken relationships described in Genesis 3—between man and himself (guilt, verse 7), between man and God (fear, verses 8-10) between man and woman (blame, verse 12), and between man and his environment (curse, verses 17-19). God had to expel Adam and Eve from the Garden of Eden. Because of the barrier of sin (see Isa. 59:2), He could no longer meet with humanity face-to-face on the Sabbath. Yet the Sabbath remained. More than ever man needed a special time to fellowship with God and meditate upon His character and works. Though as sinners human beings could not endure the glory of open encounter with their Creator, God still called for them to come and meet with Him on the Sabbath. The seventh day was still blessed, holy time. However, because God no longer appeared visibly to man on the Sabbath, the seventh day appeared externally the same as the other six. Thus it became a special test of humanity's willingness to obey God. We will look at this further in the next chapter.

Except for the sixth, the Genesis account of the patriarchs does not explicitly mention the Sabbath or any of the rest of the Ten Commandments. We should not expect to find this surprising in a succinct narrative covering several thousand years of history. Its observance is assumed and not at issue, just as during the 500-year period from Moses to David when Scripture again does not mention the Sabbath. No doubt the Sabbath comprised part of what God called "my commandments, my statutes, and my laws" (Gen. 26:5, RSV), which He commended Abraham for obeying. In Genesis numerous references to the weekly cycle (Gen. 7:4, 10; 8:10, 12; 29:26-28; 50:10) hint at a knowledge of the Sabbath, since one could know the week only by its termination at the Sabbath.[13]

During their enslavement in Egypt Pharaoh apparently forbade the people of Israel to observe the Sabbath; and when Moses, under divine direction to lead Israel out of bondage, returned from 40 years in Midian he seems to have promptly encouraged the people to again begin worshiping on the Sabbath. The Egyptian ruler protested vehemently to Moses: "Look, the people of the land are now numerous, and you are stopping them [literally, causing them to *shābat*] from working" (Ex. 5:4). God brought out His people with a mighty hand, and a major reason for the deliverance was "that they might keep his precepts and observe his laws" (Ps. 105:45). In the account of the provision of the manna in Exodus 16, God began to teach those who had left slavery and nonobservance of the Sabbath how to rest on the seventh day, and He emphasized that the Sabbath is a gift to man (Ex. 16:29). At the same time, the context of the story proclaims the Sabbath as part of God's "commandments and [His] laws" (Ex. 16:28, RSV), already in existence before the giving of manna and even before the formal announcement of the Ten Commandments from Mount Sinai.[14]

We have traveled swiftly from Creation to Sinai, but Sinai returns us to Creation. As God speaks the fourth commandment amid the thunderings and lightnings of the divine theophany, and later writes it with His own finger on tables of stone, the same reason for its observance

A Song of Creation

becomes evident as in the beginning. The Sabbath at Sinai still has its roots in Creation. Sinai tells man to remember that the Sabbath originated in the Garden of Eden, as God Himself, the Mighty Exemplar, rested, blessed, and sanctified it.

Remember the Sabbath day by keeping it holy. Six days you shall labor and do all your work, but the seventh day is a Sabbath to the Lord your God. On it you shall not do any work, neither you, nor your son or daughter, nor your manservant or maidservant, nor your animals, nor the alien within your gates. For in six days the Lord made the heavens and the earth, the sea, and all that is in them, but he rested on the seventh day. Therefore the Lord blessed the Sabbath day and made it holy (Ex. 20:8-11).

At Sinai the Sabbath became part of a codified law, the Decalogue. The Decalogue, or "ten words," formed the basis of the Sinaitic covenant the Lord made with the people of Israel about 1450 B.C. Does this mean that the Sabbath thereby became part of a legalistic code for Israel that is no longer valid for Christians "under grace"? To begin with, the fact that the Sabbath in the fourth commandment arises out of *Creation*—in the beginning, before sin and before a nation of Israel existed—should immediately alert us to the erroneousness of such a thought.

The immediate context of the Ten Commandments, also makes clear that they do not belong to a legalistic system opposed to grace. As a boy I was taught the Ten Commandments beginning with Exodus 20:3: "You shall have no other gods before me." But the introduction in verses 1 and 2 is crucial: "And God spoke all these words: 'I am the Lord your God, who brought you out of Egypt, out of the land of slavery.'"

Do you catch the significance? God says He has *already* saved His people. They have already been saved by the blood of a lamb! (see Ex. 12:1-13). The law is not for Israel to keep *in order to* be saved, but for those who are *already* saved by grace! It is not a legalistic code of requirements that we must fulfill so that God will accept us. Rather, it is a statement of an intimate covenant relationship between God and His people, a description of the abundant life for Israel in fellowship with their Redeemer. We will discuss the redemptive motivation of the Sabbath in more detail in the next chapter, but here let it be plain that the Ten Commandments, including the fourth, are not a code of legalism in opposition to the life of grace.

In the setting of Exodus 20:2, the Decalogue is nothing less than a tenfold promise of life in a covenant relationship with the God of the universe. This is true in the sense that under grace "All His biddings are enablings."[15] But it is also embedded in the very grammatical structure of the Decalogue. While it is possible to interpret the commandments as prohibitions, we can also interpret them as divine promises. For those redeemed by the blood of the Lamb, it is no longer the command "You may not have any other gods before Me," but instead, the promise "You will not have any other gods before Me. You will not make any graven images, you will not take My name in vain. I promise you! You will no longer want to do those things that interrupt our intimate personal relationship."

The grammatical form of the fourth commandment can also move beyond the emphatic imperative "Remember the Sabbath day."[16] We can also render it as a statement of an emphatic promise—"You will most certainly remember — I promise you!"[17] Here is warm covenant-promise love, not cold legalistic prohibition.

Of course, the Decalogue *can* become a legalistic code for those who think that by observing the commandments they can earn favor with God. Initially that even seems to have been the case with the Israelites at Mount Sinai. Though blood ratified the covenant, pointing to the grace of the Substitute, the people apparently thought they could obey the law by themselves. As Moses communed with God on the mountain, they fell into apostasy and learned by

A Song of Creation

bitter experience their own sinfulness and need of a Saviour. God then gave Moses details regarding the plan of salvation as foreshadowed by the sanctuary and the sacrificial system, and the people joyfully accepted God's provision of grace.

Throughout the remainder of God's instructions to him at Sinai, and again in Moses' farewell speech to Israel on the borders of the Promised Land, the pattern is always the same. First comes the mention of redemption, then law. "I have redeemed you," He says, "therefore keep My laws" (see Deut. 7:7, 11; 10:20-22, 11:1, 7, 8).

In fact, the whole book of Deuteronomy is structured along lines that emphasize the primacy of grace as the setting for law. Recently scholars have uncovered ancient treaties, or covenants, from about the time of Moses that Hittite overlords (suzerains) made with their subordinate (or vassal) states. The external form of the Hittite suzerainty treaty went as follows:[18]

1. *Preamble*—the suzerain identifies himself.
2. *Historical prologue*—description of previous relationship between suzerain and vassal, stressing the benevolence and generosity of the suzerain in the past as a basis for the vassal's gratitude and future obedience.
3. *Stipulations*—the basic and detailed obligations laid on the vassal by the suzerain, calling for commitment of loyalty by the vassal to the suzerain and establishing a covenant relationship between the two.
4. *Document clause*—statement about the preservation of the treaty in the vassal's sanctuary and provision for periodic public readings of the treaty.
5. *Witnesses*—list of gods (particularly of the suzerain) and inanimate objects—anything beyond change—who are witnesses to the making of the treaty.
6. *Blessings and curses*—the call for faithfulness and loyalty, with promises of blessings for compliance and curses for breach of confidence.

A LOVE SONG FOR THE SABBATH

What is unique about such political treaties, when we compare them with those from other periods of history, is the element of grace. After the suzerain identifies himself, he immediately describes his earlier relations with the vassal and the past benefactions that he has bestowed upon him. The ruler's recital of previous acts of grace forms the basis for what follows, the treaty stipulations, or laws. The vassal's obedience flows from gratitude for what the suzerain has already done for him. Furthermore, the ruler promises blessing for the loyal vassal.

In contrast to this kind of "treaty of grace," the Assyrian treaties of the first millennium before Christ had no historical prologue of past benefits—the Assyrians did no acts of grace, but ruled by brute force and cruel tyranny. Likewise, they offered no blessing for obedience, only curses for disloyalty.

Did God perhaps lead the ancient Near Eastern world to devise a kind of national treaty in Moses' day that would serve as an illustration of the relationship of grace and law? In any case, the book of Deuteronomy has many parallels to the formal elements of the Hittite treaty.[19] We may diagram the covenant renewal structure of Deuteronomy as follows:

1. *Preamble:* Deut. 1:1-6a
2. *Historical Prologue:* Deut. 1:6b—4:49
3. *Stipulations:* (General) Deut. 5-11
4. *Document Clause:* (Deposit) Deut. 10:5; 31:9, 24-26, (Reading) Deut. 31:10, 11
5. *Witnesses:* Deut. 30:19; 31:19; 32:1
6. *Blessings and Curses:* Deut. 11:26-32; 27-28; 33.

Note that immediately after the introduction of God, the suzerain, Moses, His spokesman, gives a detailed prologue stressing God's benevolence and grace in redeeming Israel. Only after it has laid a foundation of the prior grace of God does Deuteronomy introduce the law. The message to Israel is clear: obedience is not a prerequisite to winning God's favor; rather, it flows spontaneously out of gratitude to the

A Song of Creation

One who has already bestowed His saving grace. And the bountiful blessings of God will continually shower upon those who remain in covenant loyalty to Him.

The Old Testament prophets consistently affirmed that grace does not abolish, but rather upholds, the law.[20] They also indicate that the coming Messiah, the Christ, would maintain the same position. Isaiah predicted that the Messiah's work would be "to make his [God's] law great and glorious" (Isa. 42:21). In the psalmist's prediction of the Messiah's incarnation, we read the words that would be on His lips when He came into the world:

Here I am, I have come —
it is written about me in the scroll.
I desire to do your will, O my God;
your law is within my heart
(Ps. 40:7, 8; cf. Heb. 10:5-9).

When Jesus arrived and, as the anointed Messiah, the Christ, began His teaching ministry, He made it clear that His appearance established, not abolished, the law:

Do not think that I have come to abolish the Law or the Prophets; I have not come to abolish them but to fulfill them. I tell you the truth, until heaven and earth disappear, not the smallest letter, not the least stroke of a pen, will by any means disappear from the Law until everything is accomplished. Anyone who breaks one of the least of these commandments and teaches others to do the same will be called least in the kingdom of heaven, but whoever practices and teaches these commands will be called great in the kingdom of heaven" (Matt. 5:17-19).

Rather than repealing the Ten Commandments, Jesus, in the Sermon on the Mount, cites several of them, magnify their meaning and revealing their true original intention.[21]

Paul's teaching likewise upholds the law. He says to the

A LOVE SONG FOR THE SABBATH

Romans: "Do we, then, nullify the law by this faith? Not at all! Rather, we uphold the law" (Rom. 3:31).

Again in the same Epistle:

> What shall we say, then? Is the law sin? Certainly not! Indeed I would not have known what sin was except through the law. For I would not have known what it was to covet if the law had not said, "Do not covet". . . . So then, the law is holy, and the commandment is holy, righteous and good. . . . We know that the law is spiritual (Rom. 7:7-14).

What Paul attacked was not the law, but its legalistic perversion by those who thought that they had to earn salvation through keeping it.[22] Just as in the Old Testament, so in the New—"No one is justified before God by the law (Gal. 3:11)." In the same manner that Abraham "believed God, and it was credited to him as righteousness" (Gal. 3:6, citing Gen. 15:6), so in New Testament times man is justified by faith. But as in the Old Testament, we whom God saves by grace will be empowered by the Holy Spirit for obedience so that "the righteous requirements of the law might be fully met in us, who do not live according to the sinful nature but according to the Spirit" (Rom. 8:4, cf. Eze. 36:26, 27). As J. H. Gerstner puts it: "The coming of the Saviour did not liberate Paul *from* the law, but *to* the law. In fact, for the first time he was able to keep it (cf. Rom. 8:18)."[23] In the Epistle to the Hebrews, the apostle indicates that it is the *same law* that forms the basis of the new covenant promises as during Old Testament times. He cites the New Covenant promise of Jeremiah 31 in both Hebrew 8 and 10: "This is the covenant I will make with the house of Israel after that time, declares the Lord. I will put my laws in their minds and write them on their hearts" (Heb. 8:10).

At the same time the apostle does recognize that some laws—those pertaining to the sacrifices and the sanctuary—were types pointing forward to the life, work, and death of the Messiah. The author of Hebrews points out that according to the prediction in Psalm 40:6-8, all the typical sacrifices would culminate in the great once-for-all sacrifice of the Messiah (see Heb. 10:5).[24] Likewise, according to other Old Testament statements (Ex. 25:40 and Ps. 110:4), the earthly sanctuary services would coalesce in the high-priestly ministry of Christ in the heavenly sanctuary.[25] Thus such shadows met their substance, their natural statute of limitations, in the great Antitype. But obviously the Sabbath, originating in Eden before sin and before the institution of the sacrificial system, did not fall under this statute of limitations. The apostle quickly points out the Creation origin of the Sabbath and its continuing validity. He cites the Creation account: "And on the seventh day God rested from all his work" (cf. Heb. 4:4; Gen. 2:2, 3) and a few verses later concludes: "There remains, then, a Sabbath-rest for the people of God" (verse 9). We will further explore the rich meaning of this passage in the next chapter.

When we move to the apostle James, we find the same insistence upon the continuing validity of the law.

> But the man who looks intently into the perfect law that gives freedom, and continues to do this, not forgetting what he has heard, but doing it—he will be blessed in what he does. . . . If you really keep the royal law found in Scripture, "Love your neighbor as yourself," you are doing right. But if you show favoritism, you sin and are convicted by the law as lawbreakers. For whoever keeps the whole law and yet stumbles at just one point is guilty of breaking all of it. For he who said, "Do not commit adultery," also said, "Do not murder." If you do not commit adultery but do commit murder, you have become a lawbreaker. Speak and act as those who are going to be judged by the law that gives freedom (James 1:25; 2:8-12).

A LOVE SONG FOR THE SABBATH

Note that for James, the law is the "law that gives freedom," the "royal law."

The testimony of the apostle John is just as clear:

> This is how we know that we love the children of God: by loving God and carrying out his commands. This is love for God: to obey his commands. And his commands are not burdensome (1 John 5:2, 3).

> This calls for patient endurance on the part of the saints who obey God's commandments and remain faithful to Jesus (Rev. 14:12).

Numerous recent scholars, including prominent Evangelicals who do not (yet!) observe the seventh-day Sabbath, are coming to realize that grace does not abolish but rather maintains and upholds the law.

Regarding Christ and the law, Gerstner writes:

> Christ's affirmation of the moral law was complete. Rather than setting His disciples free from the law, He tied them more tightly to it. He abrogated not one commandment but instead intensified all. . . . Christ fulfilled the moral law by obeying it and showing its intense spirituality, thus establishing it on a surer basis than ever as the eternal law of righteousness.[26]

Gerstner also comments on Paul's position:

> The major development of the New Testament concept of law is found in the writings of Paul. Like Christ, he reaffirmed the law and explicated the relationship between law and grace. . . . Paul's basic principle was that Christ is not the negation of the law, but the fulfillment of it. . . . He showed that grace leads again to law. . . . The Christian lives in obedience to the law, not in merit from it. . . . So far was Paul from negating the law that he would not allow

A Song of Creation

Christians to act in cases where the teaching of the law seemed unclear unless they believed that the law favored their course of action, because 'whatsoever is not of faith, is sin.' . . . The coming of the Saviour did not liberate Paul from the law, but to the law. In fact, for the first time he was able to keep it (cf. Rom. 8:1-4).[27]

Summarizing the view of other New Testament writers, Gerstner concludes:

> While the remainder of the New Testament is not so full in its treatment, it seems to follow the pattern of teaching found in Christ and Paul.[28]

What is true about the permanence of the law in general also applies to the Sabbath commandment in particular. More and more are recognizing that the Sabbath has its roots in Creation and is therefore for all people of all times, not just for the Jews of the Old Testament.

In his recent article on the Sabbath in the *New International Dictionary of New Testament Theology* W. Stott cites Genesis 2:3 ("God blessed the seventh day and made it holy,") with the following commentary:

> As the Creation story in Genesis 1 centers on the creation of man on the sixth day, the author evidently intends the inauguration of the Sabbath to be seen as the climax of the creation process as it applied to the man who had been formed (B. S. Childs, *Exodus,* 1974, 416). As Eichrodt has pointed out, this shows that the day was regarded as a source of blessing of universal significance and not merely for Israel, and as being coeval with the human race (W. Eichrodt, *Theology of the Old Testament,* I, *1961, 133).*[29]

Stott then describes the Old Testament perspective on

the Sabbath: "To summarize, the Old Testament attitude to the Sabbath was to regard it as a divine ordinance which was universal, but especially relevant to Israel as a redeemed people."[30]

Stott also acknowledges that Jesus Himself grounds the Sabbath in Creation and thus upholds its universal, abiding character:

> Turning now to Mark 2:27 ["The Sabbath was made for man, not man for the Sabbath. So the Son of Man is Lord even of the Sabbath"], there is a positive statement of Christ's about the Sabbath. Here its institution is stated to have been made for man's good, and it would seem that there is at least an indirect reference to the account in Gen. 2:1, 2 (J. Jeremias, *New Testament Theology*, I, 1971, 208). It would then imply that the ordinance was not merely for Israel, but had a pre-Israelite, worldwide, humanitarian implication. This is followed by the claim, mentioned in the other two Gospels, that Jesus was "Lord of the Sabbath." In other words, He has the authority to decide about its observance. Far from suggesting that, though a benefit to man, it was to be annulled, it would suggest that the manner of its observance was under the control of Christ himself.[31]

Gerstner, in his article "Law in the New Testament," in the *International Standard Bible Encyclopedia*, comes to the same conclusion regarding this passage:

> Although many regard this teaching as tantamount to a rejection of the Mosiac law, Christ actually affirmed the Sabbath by saying that it was made not just for the Jews but for mankind, and was made not for one time but for all time, presumably.[32]

Unfortunately, many of the recent authors who have recognized the Creation basis for the Sabbath and have

A Song of Creation

acknowledged its abiding validity still do not accept the seventh-day Sabbath because, as they argue, it is only the principle of "one day in seven" that is important, not the precise seventh day (Saturday). But what we have learned about God's "palace in time," erected in Eden, shows us the crucial importance of *the* seventh day, not just *a* seventh day. God blessed and sanctified not any or all days, but one specific day—the seventh. Only it was set apart by God for a special use—for Him to enter into fellowship with humanity on it. It is His specially appointed all-day date with us.

I remember those first all-day dates I had with the one who would later become my wife. All week I lived for the chance to spend an entire day with the person I loved. Not for the world would I have missed that appointment by arriving on the wrong day!

God has arranged a special day of communion with man—the holy seventh-day Sabbath. Who would want to miss His holy presence by showing up on the wrong day? He even scheduled His all-day date to begin at the most opportune time of day. The Creator didn't start the Sabbath at midnight, when we would be asleep, or in the early morning, when we are still drowsy. Rather, God ordained the Sabbath to begin in the cool of the day, at sunset (see Lev. 23:32; Mark 1:32), when we are most receptive to a refreshing pause, most eager for a time of intimate fellowship and joyous celebration. Who would want to miss even part of that divine appointment by deciding to meet it at another time?

God has arranged to meet with us on the birthday of the world. It is His "weekaversary" celebration with us. My own birthday is on June 6 for keeps, no matter how much I would rather change it to another day. And my wedding anniversary will always fall on July 28, no matter how often during July camp meetings and pastors' conventions my wife and I have wished it were another month. (We finally celebrated it by ourselves this year for the first time since we have been married.) I can't change my birthday as long as I live, and likewise the birthday of the world will never shift to another day as long as the world exists. My wife and I can't change our anniversary date as long as we are married—and we have covenanted that to be forever. Likewise, God's weekaversary celebration will remain the same as long as He chooses to enter into covenant fellowship with humanity—and that, He has promised, will be forever!

Creation and the Meaning of Life

Now we can begin to sense the crucial importance of rooting the Sabbath in Creation. Creation provides the ultimate foundation for the universal and eternal observance of the Sabbath on our planet. Sabbath is a memorial of Creation, and the meaning of the Sabbath is bound up in Creation. In our song for the Sabbath (Ps. 92:4-6), we have seen that Creation provides the foundational motivation for joy on the Sabbath. As we fellowship with God and meditate on His works, we cannot help bursting forth into joyous praise.

Thus as on the Sabbath we memorialize Creation, we find not only the universal, abiding roots of the Sabbath and the ground of Sabbath joy, but also the basic orientation for our whole lives in all our multifaceted relationships. We see, first, who God is—our transcendant Creator and personal Lover, one infinitely worthy of our trust, one who respects our own freedom. Second, we encounter who we really are—creatures in absolute dependence upon our Creator, yet deeply loved by Him, made in His image, worthwhile children of God.

Third, we discover our appropriate relationship to God. As we accept God as the transcendent and omnipotent Creator, we are willing to accept our own creatureliness and surrender our claim to be masters of our fate. Such a relationship provides a sure antidote to human pride. At the same time, it establishes the fundamental basis of a healthy self-esteem. God values us, and He loves to enter into personal relationship with us.

A Song of Creation

Fourth, on the Sabbath we view our proper relationship with other people. We are all of one blood in Adam, brothers and sisters in the great web of the human family. The Creation is the great leveler, showing that all—men and women, rich and poor, Black and White—have been made equally in the image of God. And God created us with a purpose in life—a purpose fulfilled in relationships, companionship, and love.

Fifth, the Sabbath grounded in Creation clarifies our relationship with our environment. We learn—contrary to the belief of an ancient heresy—that God created matter good, to be enjoyed as His gifts. Enjoyed, but not exploited. Man received dominion over his environment as stewards to serve and protect it. Exodus 23:12 underscores the humanitarian function of the Sabbath: "that your ox and your donkey may rest."

Sixth, the Creation Sabbath puts work into proper perspective. The Creator meant labor to have dignity —"Six days [you shall] do your work"—and the goals of productivity are considered worthy ones. Yet the Creation-rooted Sabbath reminds man not to place ultimate confidence in his work, not to become intoxicated with his own productivity, not to become a slave to toil. The first Sabbath was Adam and Eve's first full day of existence. They had not yet worked, and came to the Sabbath with nothing of their own hands to offer—except their fellowship and loyalty. Free from any need to merit God's favor by some work of their own, they welcomed His divine gift of grace—His own presence in the Sabbath.

Finally, the Sabbath in Creation reveals the true basis and meaning of worship. The call to worship God rises out of the fact that He is the Creator. Worship is a shortened form of *worthship.* On the Sabbath man discovers the worth of His Creator and his own worth, and his heart and soul go out spontaneously in adoration and praise. In short, the Creation Sabbath embraces the Creator's purpose for His creatures—everything He wants us to be to Him and everything He wants to be to us.

A LOVE SONG FOR THE SABBATH

Creation Under Fire

Because God's creatorship and our creatureliness are a fundamental part of reality, this fact has come under special attack in the cosmic conflict between good and evil. Modern man has been so anxious to grasp for autonomy that he has been willing to lower himself to a common origin with the brutes of earth. Interestingly, Psalm 92:6 states regarding Creation (in literal translation): "The *brute-man* cannot know, the fool cannot understand this."[33]

According to one recent count, some 480,000 earth and life scientists in the U.S.A. trace man's origin from lower forms of life through the evolutionary process, while only a mere 700 or so with respectable academic credentials still hold to a literal reading of the biblical record in its description of a Special Creation.[34] But the Scriptures challenge us to keep solid our anchor of Creation and a personal Creator. This issue is of particular concern because without a literal seven-day creation, the Seventh-day Sabbath as a memorial of Creation has lost its historical moorings.

As I write these lines, I have just returned from a 10-day geological field conference held in southwest Utah. That area of the U.S.A. is the only location in the world where within a radius of a few hours' drive one can examine virtually the entire geological column from the Pre-Cambrian up to the Cenozoic. In the conference we witnessed major problems that question an evolutionary interpretation of the fossil record. I was encouraged to see the emergence of impressive evidence supporting a recent creation of life and a global deluge rather than the theory of evolution.[35]

That does not mean that anyone proved a creationistic understanding of origins. The conference was careful to point out to us that there are some remaining problems in interpreting the fossil record from the perspective of a sudden emergence of life on earth at the hand of a Master Designer. The scientific data is not all in. So little work has been done with a view toward establishing an alternative model to evolution. With only a handful of scientists

A Song of Creation

studying the data from a creationist viewpoint, and a whole army examining it within an evolutionary framework, it is something like David fighting Goliath. But some scientists are daring to look at the data in light of the biblical perspective. Interestingly, in recent years a number of eminent scientists who do not accept the biblical position are nonetheless raising pointed questions concerning the validity of the evolutionary hypothesis.[36]

Looking at both the scientific evidence and the biblical data has reaffirmed my conviction that the Bible and science, rightly interpreted, do not contradict but rather illuminate each other. The scriptural record is clear. The fourth commandment (Ex. 20:8-11) indicates by direct parallel that the first seven days were literal 24-hour days, like the present weekly cycle. Just as God created the heavens and the earth in six days and rested the seventh, so man has the first six days of the week for work and the seventh for rest.

The Genesis account itself gives abundant evidence that the author intended his audience to take it literally. First, each day of Creation consisted of an evening and a morning (see Gen. 1:5, 8, 13, 19, 23, 31). Second, he labeled each day with an ordinal number ("first," "second," etc.), and elsewhere in Scripture the usage of *day* with the ordinal consistently refers to a *literal* day. Third, the seven-day Creation account concludes with this clause: "These are the generations of the heavens and the earth when they were created" (Gen. 2:4, KJV). The word *toledoth* ("generations") here is a technical term used in the setting of genealogies that seek to depict time and history. The author of Genesis also employs *toledoth* in connection with each of the succeeding sections of Genesis. Thus *toledoth* in Genesis 2:4 indicates that the account of Creation should be taken just as literally as the rest of the Genesis narratives.[37]

Beyond the Genesis evidence, later Old Testament writers concur that Creation was by divine fiat: "By the word of the Lord were the heavens made, their starry host by the breath of his mouth. . . . For he spoke, and it came to be; he commanded, and it stood firm" (Ps. 33:6, 9; see also Ps. 104). The Old Testament prophets refer repeatedly to a literal creation by God as His ultimate claim to worship and reverence.[38] Likewise, in the New Testament, Jesus and all New Testament writers except James refer affirmatively to Genesis 1-11 as a historically reliable account.[39]

The psalmist of the Sabbath declared: "How great are your works, O Lord, how profound your thoughts." (Ps. 92:5).

Let us contemplate—particularly on the Sabbath—the greatness of His works; let us seek to plumb the depths of His thoughts. And let the truth of our creation by a loving and caring God, memorialized by the Seventh-day Sabbath, be our solid conviction and motivation for humility, trust, and joy.

Singing the Creation Song

Some of my fondest boyhood memories come from when our family entered experientially into the Sabbath song of Creation. I still treasure those Friday evenings when we sat on the backyard lawn swing, watching the sunset to the accompaniment of "Day Is Dying in the West" and then gazing at the moon, planets, and stars through my brother's homemade telescope. Those Sabbath afternoons spent at Fish Canyon, watching the pink salamanders in Fish Creek and feeling the spray of the thundering Fish Canyon Falls. Those moments of Sabbath majesty spent in a lonely stretch of Pismo Beach, sensing the awesome power of God in the pounding surf. Those occasions of Sabbath ecstasy atop Mount San Jacinto or Mount Pacifico that called forth the words of the song:

How big is God!
How great and wide His vast domain.
To try and tell
These lips can only start.

Or those moments we spent over a magnifying glass,

A Song of Creation

examining the complex structure of a minute insect that reminded us of the rest of the song:

> Yet small enough
> To live within my heart.

Now I have a family of my own, and until our move a year ago, we lived about a mile from church. On pleasant Sabbaths, and even sometimes in blustery weather, we loved to walk briskly along the flower-lined lanes to church. We mused on how the flowers have no real utilitarian purpose—except as God's gift of love to gladden the human heart. The robins, sparrows, and cardinals joined with our voices while we praised God in song. As we approached the church, the chimes rang out across the neighborhood, flooding our hearts with joy. After the morning services, we took a more leisurely pace, stopping to pick bouquets of wildflowers, watching a robin build a nest, collecting leaves from all the different trees we passed. All the flowers, the birds, the trees, seemed to resound with messages of God's power, wisdom, and love.

Now that we've moved farther away, we usually take our nature excursions in the afternoon (although last week, with my family visiting relatives, I experienced the exhilaration of canoeing downstream to church and back). We love to walk along the stream and through the woods behind our house, or saunter through the orchard next door when the blossoms are in full bloom. As we go along, we identify or collect specimens of flora or fauna, or just pick up pretty stones from the rock pile down the road. Sometimes we play Bible nature games—utilizing props from our nature adventures to tell a Bible story, or finding things in nature mentioned in the Bible. Other times we think of spiritual lessons that the various objects in nature teach, or discuss particular characteristics of God that the creatures we encounter on our walks remind us of. It's great to celebrate God's creation!

A LOVE SONG FOR THE SABBATH

We're just beginning to unlock the wonders of God's love that nature's 10,000 voices have to teach us. Recently we have discovered several delightful books with a multitude of creative ideas for making our Sabbaths in nature more and more of an exquisite delight.[40]

May I encourage you to take time to sing the Sabbath song of Creation. Even if you live in the city, you can find patches of natural surroundings, or at least pictures of them. On rainy days you can study what Scripture and Ellen G. White teach about the Creator and the lessons to be learned from His marvelous works.

God is waiting to meet with you, to fellowship and celebrate with you. On the Sabbath date with Him, you can forget your unfinished work from the weekdays and enter into His rest. Particularly as you encounter Him in the things of nature, your senses will be enraptured; you won't be able to help yourself—you will break forth in a song of love and praise. Let the love song for the Sabbath and the God of the Sabbath well up in your heart—and let it ring out!

> O Lord, with joy my heart expands
> Before the wonders of Thy hands;
> Great works, Jehovah, Thou hast wrought,
> Exceeding deep Thine every thought;
> A foolish man knows not their worth,
> Nor he whose mind is of the earth.
> (Ps. 92: 4-6, paraphrase).

References

[1] Heschel develops this concept in *The Sabbath*, pp. 12-24.

[2] Brown, Driver, and Briggs, *A Hebrew and English Lexicon of the Old Testament*, p. 991; W. Stott, "Sabbath, Lord's Day," in Colin Brown, ed., *The New International Dictionary of New Testament Theology* (Grand Rapids: Zondervan, 1978), vol. 3, p. 405.

[3] Heschel, p. 22; cf. L. J. Coppes, "*nuah*," in Harris, *Theological Wordbook of the Old Testament*, vol. 2, pp. 562, 563.

[4] See Brown, Driver, and Briggs, p. 661.

[5] D. W. Thomas, ed., *Documents From Old Testament Times* (New York: Harper and Row, 1958), p. 12.

[6] See J. N. Oswalt, "barak," in Harris, vol. 1, p. 132, and bibliography cited by Oswalt.

A Song of Creation

[7] See Brown, Driver, and Briggs, p. 871; Thomas E. McComiskey, "*qādash*," in Harris, vol. 2, pp. 786-789.

[8] Heschel, p. 82.

[9] See J. Muilenburg, "Holiness," in G. A. Buttrick, ed., *Interpreter's Dictionary of the Bible* (New York: Abingdon Press, 1962), vol. 2, pp. 616-623; Nilton Amorim, "Desecration and Defilement in the Old Testament." (Ph.D. diss., Andrews University, Berrien Springs, Michigan, 1985), pp. 147-161.

[10] Heschel, p. 18.

[11] Philo *Moses* 1. 37; *On the Creation* 30; *The Special Laws*, 2. 15. 16.

[12] James Weldon Johnson, *God's Trombones* (New York: The Viking Press, 1927), pp. 17-20.

[13] For a fuller discussion of this period, see J. N. Andrews, *History of the Sabbath and First Day of the Week*, 2nd ed. (Battle Creek, Mich.: SDA Pub. Assn., 1873), pp. 28-32.

[14] See the discussion by Gerhard Hasel, "The Sabbath in the Pentateuch," in Strand, *The Sabbath in Scripture and History*, pp. 26, 27.

[15] Ellen G. White, *Christ's Object Lessons* (Mountain View, Calif.: Pacific Press Pub. Assn., 1941), p. 333.

[16] E. Kautzsch, ed., *Gesenius' Hebrew Grammar* (Oxford: Clarendon, 1910), par. 113bb.

[17] *Ibid.*, par. 113ee.

[18] For further discussion, see Meredith Kline, *Treaty of the Great King: The Covenant Structure of Deuteronomy* (Grand Rapids: William B. Eerdmans, 1983).

[19] See Kline; Kenneth Kitchen, *Ancient Orient and Old Testament* (Downers Grove, Ill.: InterVarsity, 1966), pp. 90-102; Peter Craigie, *The New International Commentary of the Old Testament: Deuteronomy* (Grand Rapids: William B. Eerdmans, 1976), pp. 36-45.

[20] See R. V. Bergren, *The Prophets and the Law* (Cincinnati: Jewish Institute of Religion, 1974).

[21] See J. H. Gerstner, "Law in the New Testament," in G. W. Bromiley et al., eds., *The International Standard Bible Encyclopedia* (Grand Rapids: William B. Eerdmans, 1979), vol. 3, pp. 86-88.

[22] *Ibid.*, pp. 88-91.

[23] *Ibid.*, p. 90.

[24] See Richard M. Davidson, "Typology and the Levitical System," *Ministry*, April 1984, pp. 11, 12.

[25] *Ibid.*

[26] Gerstner, p. 88.

[27] *Ibid.*, pp. 89-90.

[28] *Ibid.*, p. 91.

[29] Stott, p. 406.

[30] *Ibid.*, p. 407.

[31] *Ibid.*, p. 410.

[32] Gerstner, p. 86.

[33] In light of the poetic stanza divisions and parallels with the usage of the word *this* in other psalms to refer to what precedes, not what follows (see Derek Kidner, *Psalms 73-150: A Commentary*, in D. J. Wiseman, ed., *Tyndale Old Testament Commentaries* [Downers Grove, Ill.: InterVarsity Press, 1975], p. 335), this sentence more accurately refers to verses 4, 5, and not to verse 7, as in some modern translations.

[34] See *Newsweek*, June 29, 1987, p. 23.

A LOVE SONG FOR THE SABBATH

[35] For a summary of recent findings in layman's terminology, see Harold Coffin with R. H. Brown, *Origin by Design* (Washington, D.C.: Review and Herald Pub. Assn., 1983) and other material available upon request from the Geoscience Research Institute, Loma Linda University, Loma Linda, CA 92350.

[36] See especially Michael Denton, *Evolution: A Theory in Crisis* (Bethesda, Md.: Adler and Adler, 1986); cf. Francis Hitching, *The Neck of the Giraffe* (New Haven, Conn.: Ticknor and Fields, 1982); G. A. Kerut, *Implications of Evolution* (New York: Pergamon Press, 1960); Tom Bethell, "Agnostic Evolutionists: The Taxonomic Case Against Darwin," *Harper's*, Feb. 1985, pp. 49-61; Mae-Wan Ho and Peter T. Saunders, eds., *Beyond Neo-Darwinism* (London: Academic Press, 1984); Paul S. Moorhead and Martin M. Kaplan, eds., *Mathematical Challenges to the Neo-Darwinian Interpretation of Evolution* (Philadelphia: Wistar Institute Press, 1967).

[37] See Jacques Doukhan, *The Genesis Creation Story: Its Literary Structure* (Berrien Springs, Mich.: Andrews University Press, 1978), pp. 174-182.

[38] See, e.g., Isa. 40:25, 26; 45:18; cf. Ps. 100:3; 95:6.

[39] Matt. 19:4, 5; 24:37-39; Mark 10:6; Luke 3:38; 17:26, 27; Rom. 5:12; 1 Cor. 6:16; 11:8, 9, 12; 15:21, 22, 45; 2 Cor. 11:3; Eph. 5:31; 1 Tim. 2:13, 14; Heb. 11:7; 1 Peter 3:20; 2 Peter 2:5; 3:4-6; 1 John 3:12; Jude 11, 14; Rev. 14:7.

[40] See especially Eileen E. Lantry, *A Family Guide to Sabbath Nature Activities* (Mountain View, Calif.: Pacific Press Pub. Assn., 1980) and her extensive bibliography of nature books, pp. 120-124; see also *Character Sketches: From the Pages of Scripture Illustrated in the World of Nature*, vols. 1, 2 (Rand McNally for the Institute in Basic Youth Conflicts, 1978); and Gerita Garver Liebelt, *From Dilemma to Delight: Creative Ideas for Happy Sabbaths* (Washington, D.C.: Review and Herald Pub. Assn., 1986), pp. 60-75.

Chapter 4

A Song of Redemption

Though the wicked spring up like grass
And all evildoers flourish,
They will be forever destroyed.

But you, O Lord, are exalted forever.

For surely your enemies, O Lord,
surely your enemies will perish;
all evildoers will be scattered.

—Ps. 92:7-9

This central stanza of our love song for the Sabbath leads us into the second motivation for joy on the Sabbath. Here we see that the Sabbath is not only a celebration of Creation but also of redemption. Verse 7 focuses on redemption in the past, verse 9 points us to future redemption, and verse 8, the one-line apex to the whole psalm, highlights the fundamental issue in the plan of redemption and the meaning of the Sabbath. Come, let us sing a song of redemption!

Redemption Past

Although some English versions translate verse 7 in the future tense, the most precise rendering refers to a particular event that has taken place in the past, as captured in the NASB and other modern translations:[1]

A LOVE SONG FOR THE SABBATH

When the wicked sprouted up like grass,
And all the workers of iniquity flourished,
It came to pass that they were absolutely destroyed.

The historical event the psalmist refers to is most probably the Exodus when God delivered Israel from Egyptian bondage.[2] It was the time of God's mighty deliverance of His people—the time of Old Testament redemption par excellence. And yes, the Exodus was a time of joyous song. According to Psalm 105:43, "he led forth his people with joy, his chosen ones with singing" (RSV).

From the banks of the Red Sea there arose "the earliest song recorded in the Bible from the lips of men . . . that glorious outburst of thanksgiving by the hosts of Israel,"[3] the Song of Moses:

I will sing to the Lord,
for he is highly exalted.
The horse and its rider
he has hurled into the sea.
The Lord is my strength and my song;
he has become my salvation.
He is my God, and I will praise him,
my father's God, and I will exalt him.
(Ex. 15:1, 2).

After Moses and all Israel had sung the song of deliverance, the women took up tambourines and danced joyously, while Miriam burst forth with this climactic refrain:

Sing to the Lord,
for he is highly exalted.
The horse and its rider
he has hurled into the sea (verse 21).

Here truly was a moment of celebration, a triumph of redemption! The redemption stanza of the love song for Sabbath echoes the message and melody of the Song of

A Song of Redemption

Moses: the wicked enemy is destroyed, God is highly exalted. On Sabbath heaven invites us to join in this anthem of redemption.

What is implicit in Psalm 92 becomes explicit in the Sabbath commandment of Deuteronomy 5. On the borders of the Promised Land Moses rehearses before the people the account of God's mighty acts of redemption, and then reiterates the Ten Commandments that God proclaimed on Mount Sinai. The commandments are the same, but when Moses comes to the fourth commandment, the Lord inspires him to point out an additional dimension to the meaning of the Sabbath:

> Observe the Sabbath day by keeping it holy, as the Lord your God has commanded you. Six days you shall labor and do all your work, but the seventh day is a Sabbath to the Lord your God. On it you shall not do any work, neither you, nor your son or daughter, nor your manservant or maidservant, nor your ox, your donkey or any of your animals, nor the alien within your gates, so that your manservant and maidservant may rest, as you do. Remember that you were slaves in Egypt and that the Lord your God brought you out of there with a mighty hand and an outstretched arm. Therefore the Lord your God has commanded you to observe the Sabbath day (Deut. 5:12-15).

A careful analysis of the intricate structure of this passage[4] reveals that the introduction (verse 12) and conclusion (verse 15) form a bracket, or framework, around the commandment. The two matching parts provide the reason, or motivation, for the Sabbath commandment itself—simply that "the Lord your God has commanded you." By the reference to the Lord's prior command, given 40 years before at Mount Sinai, Moses implies the ultimate grounding of the Sabbath in Creation, as recorded in Exodus 20, without explicitly mentioning it.

A LOVE SONG FOR THE SABBATH

At the same time Moses makes clear that the Sabbath also has a redemptive aspect. On Sabbath the Israelites were even to liberate the servants from their toil. As a people, Israel could especially appreciate the redemptive feature of Sabbath rest because they had once been slaves in Egypt. But God had redeemed them with a mighty hand, and their Sabbath rest epitomized that liberation for all. Thus their Deliverer asked them to make the Sabbath a special time for remembering their own redemption. Also, on Sabbath they were to extend that redemptive work to those not yet completely free. Elsewhere the Pentateuch extends the Sabbath principle of liberation to its ultimate in the sabbatical year (every seventh year) and the jubilee (after seven sabbatical years). These yearlong Sabbaths brought permanent emancipation for slaves if they so chose (see Ex. 21:1-6; Deut. 15:1-18; Lev. 25:8-55).

The Sabbath—a memorial of redemption and freedom! Each Sabbath called for Israel to remember in a special way that God had redeemed them from bondage in Egypt, redeemed them from the threat of their enemies at the Red Sea. At the thoughtful reminder of such a great divine redemption, who could keep from singing the Song of Moses? Who could resist joining in the redemption stanza of the love song for the Sabbath?

If Israel of old burst spontaneously into melodious Sabbath praise at the thought of the Exodus from Egyptian bondage, how much more joyfully can we who are spiritual Israel chorus the love song of redemption as we contemplate the new Exodus, the cross. By His death the antitypical Lamb of God has delivered us from the bondage of sin. Redeemed by the blood of the Lamb, we have been freed from the threats of the enemy. We are free at last!

Christ's work of redemption is linked not only to the Exodus but to Creation. His work as redeemer was really an act of re-creation, of restoring in man the image of God given at Creation but lost through sin. In a special way the Sabbath ties together Christ's redemptive and creative activities. At the end of the six days of Creation, the Creator

A Song of Redemption

(Christ, John 1:1-3) finished all His work and began His Sabbath rest (Gen. 2:2). Likewise at the end of His earthly redemptive mission the Re-Creator declared on the cross, "It is finished!" (John 19:30), and entered into Sabbath rest. The Sabbath of the Garden of Eden and the Sabbath of the Garden near Golgotha stand as twin monuments to the love and work of Christ.

Far from abolishing the Sabbath by His death, even in His death Christ honored it (and along with Him, His disciples "rested . . . in obedience to the commandment" [Luke 23:56]). Jesus' own example in the New Testament places His seal upon the Sabbath as the great memorial of re-creation, just as His example in Eden made it a perpetual monument to Creation.

Our Saviour's life and ministry before the cross had already highlighted the continuing validity and redemptive (or re-creative) significance of the Sabbath. Shortly after the temptation in the wilderness, "he went to Nazareth, where he had been brought up, and on the Sabbath day he went into the synagogue, as was his custom" (Luke 4:16). In His "inaugural address" that followed, Christ announced His mission by reading from the sabbatical liberation message of Isaiah 61:1-2:

> The Spirit of the Lord is on me,
>> because he has anointed me
>> to preach good news to the poor.
> He has sent me to proclaim freedom for the prisoners
>> and recovery of sight for the blind,
>> to release the oppressed,
>> to proclaim the year of the Lord's favor
>> (Luke 4:18, 19).

After reading the Old Testament passage, Christ announced plainly, "Today this scripture is fulfilled in your hearing" (verse 21). He had come to fulfill the redemptive function of the sabbatical year.

Jesus particularly intended that those miracles of healing He performed on the Sabbath would reveal the true redemptive dimension of the Sabbath, something that by the first century A.D. had become well-nigh obliterated by the accumulation of rabbinic restrictions and regulations. Several recent studies have traced the redemption theme beautifully throughout the five Sabbath healing miracles recorded in the Gospels.[5]

Briefly, let us look at each miracle. In the passages describing the healing of the man with the withered hand (Matt. 12:9-14; Mark 3:1-6; Luke 6:6-11), Jesus pinpoints the *healing,* or *saving* (these two words are the same in Greek), purpose of the Sabbath. He asked those who sought for a reason to accuse Him, "Which is lawful on the Sabbath: to do good or to do evil, to save life or to kill?" (Mark 3:4). And by His act of healing that followed, He revealed the right answer. Notice, Jesus is not abrogating the Sabbath but clarifying its true intent. As Stott puts it in the *New International Dictionary of New Testament Theology*: "Again there is no challenge to the law itself; in fact, the wording assumes its relevance. The right use of the law, the salvation, the making whole of man, is the great object behind that law, and therefore the healing is justified."[6]

In the healing of the crippled woman, recorded in Luke 13:10-17, we can hardly consider it accidental that in the space of the three verses in the story in which Jesus speaks, He uses the same word *luein* ("to free") three times. Jesus first calls the stooped woman forward in the synagogue and tells her, "Woman, you are set free *[luein]* from your infirmity" (verse 12). After He had healed her and the synagogue ruler objected because the act occurred on Sabbath instead of one of the six working days, Jesus replied, "You hypocrites! Doesn't each of you on the Sabbath untie *[luein]* his ox or donkey from the stall and lead it out to give it water? Then should not this woman, a daughter of Abraham, whom Satan has kept bound for eighteen long years, be set free *[luein]* on the Sabbath day from what bound her?" (verse 15).

Here is a beautiful illustration of the sabbatical principle

A Song of Redemption

of liberation that Jesus had announced in His inaugural Nazareth address. To those who were willing to liberate an animal on the Sabbath so it could drink, Jesus drives the point home: how much more appropriate it is to release a suffering human being from the shackles of Satan!

The other Sabbath miracles display the same concern for restoring God's original redemptive intention for the Sabbath, rescuing it from the distortions heaped upon it by man-made regulations. When He cured the man with dropsy (Luke 14:1-6), He again asked the Pharisees and the experts in religious law whether it was right to heal on the Sabbath. Afterward He explained that healing those who are sick is just as much an act of mercy as pulling an animal out from a well. If the latter is permissable, Jesus implied, how much more should the former be encouraged!

After the incident involving the invalid at the Pool of Bethesda (John 5:1-18), Jesus replied to His accusers, "My Father is always at his work to this very day, and I, too, am working" (verse 17). In effect, Jesus said that He was continuing the very activity that the Father had been doing continuously—the work of redemption. Here again Christ is not annulling the Sabbath day, but by the words "until now," He is showing that "all the while that the Sabbath command was in force, God was, in fact, working. In other words, the Sabbath command does not mean doing nothing (*argia*), but the doing of the work of God. This was, in fact, what Christ had been doing in the healing of the infirm man."[7]

Finally, in the case of the man born blind (John 9), Jesus does not publicly defend His action of healing, but afterwards to His disciples He clarifies the redemptive purpose: "that the work of God might be displayed" (verse 13). In the Sabbath healing miracles, we have seen that Jesus was not abrogating the Sabbath. After examining the five incidents in turn, Stott, writes: "We may conclude, then, that though Jesus broke through the rabbinic traditions about the Sabbath, there was no annulling of the observance of the day."[8]

A LOVE SONG FOR THE SABBATH

John Brunt insightfully points out that in all of the Sabbath miracles Jesus purposefully sets about to heal in order to demonstrate the true meaning of the Sabbath in contrast to rabbinic distortions.[9] All of these miracles center in a controversy over the Sabbath. In all of them Jesus takes the initiative to heal, a remarkable act in light of the fact that in no other case of healing does He take such initiative—elsewhere someone else always requests the healing. Further, the healings all concern a chronic illness rather than an emergency or acute situation. Since the rabbis allowed healing of acute cases of illness on the Sabbath, Jesus' pattern of seeking out chronic cases shows that He purposely healed in order to teach a truth about the Sabbath. By asking incisive questions, He often cut through the legalistic rabbinic regulations and showed that the Sabbath is a day for healing. To heal, or to save (again the same Greek word for both, *sozein*)—here is the very essence of the Sabbath!

Jesus' Sabbath healing stories are not just accounts of people long ago and far away. The healing essence of the Sabbath is for us today as much as it was for those in the first century of the Christian Era. The healing stories can be our stories! As the sun sets on Friday evening God longs for us to sing the song of redemption and liberation not just as theological truth but as a song of experience.

Jesus specifically invites us to enter into His redemption rest, which the Sabbath symbolizes. In the context of two Sabbath episodes showing the close tie between the Sabbath and His gospel invitation,[10] Christ says, "Come to me, all you who are weary and burdened, and I will give you rest" (Matt. 11:28). Such Sabbath rest is "not merely physical relaxation but the peace and joy of His forgiveness and redemption."[11]

The author of Hebrews likewise appeals for us to experience Sabbath rest. As was the case with Jesus, we have here no question of abrogating the seventh-day Sabbath, for the apostle states explicitly, "There remains, then, a Sabbath-rest *[sabbatismos]* for the people of God" (Heb.

A Song of Redemption

4:9). Writing as he was to Christians greatly attracted to Jewish liturgy (as the rest of the Epistle makes clear), it would be unthinkable for the author to use such language if he did not assume the continuing validity of the seventh-day Sabbath.[12] The apostle exhorts his hearers—and us!—to experience the deep redemptive meaning of Sabbath rest. The rest that the seventh-day Sabbath symbolizes and epitomizes is none other than the "rest of grace."[13] It is the spiritual cessation in which man "rests from his own work, just as God did from his" (verse 10). God has completed His work of redemption in Christ, and we do not need to labor to try to earn that salvation. By faith we can simply reach out and accept the gift, and enter God's rest.

Then each week as the Sabbath begins, we can see ourselves as the ones whom Christ has made whole. We whose hands were withered and useless to earn our own salvation, we who were stooped over by the burdens of sin and pressures of life, we who had spiritual dropsy, spiritual paralysis, spiritual blindness—we've been unshackled, healed, saved, released! Naturally we cannot help leaping for joy, singing the Sabbath song of redemption!

Furthermore we will rejoice to share that experience of liberation with others. As we remember our redemption from bondage, it will motivate us to follow the course of the Old Testament and extend that liberating rest to those not yet free. Following in the footsteps of Jesus, we will make the Sabbath a day for healing.

The Sabbath and Future Redemption

Psalm 92, the song for the Sabbath, includes not only a memorial of redemption already accomplished but also a promise of ultimate future salvation. In verse 9 we read:

For surely your enemies, O Lord,
surely your enemies will perish;
all evildoers will be scattered.

What does the Sabbath have to do with the end of God's

enemies, the final climax of the struggle between good and evil? The Scriptures make it clear that the Sabbath has an integral relationship with this conflict: its observance will actually constitute an ultimate test of loyalty to God and will be a special focus of attack from God's enemies. To set the stage, let's take a broad view of the cosmic warfare between good and evil.

From a number of passages of Scripture[14] we learn that even before the creation of our world, a controversy had arisen in heaven over the character of God. Satan (then Lucifer) became jealous because the members of the Godhead had not taken him into Their counsels regarding the creation of the earth, and he accused God of being a harsh, dictatorial tyrant whose character was untrustworthy and whose law was an infringement of freedom. He alleged that no one would serve God for His own sake, but only for what they could get out of Him (see Job 1, 2).

The situation finally ripened into open war in heaven, and God had to cast Satan and his angels out (see Rev. 12:7-9). Yet serious questions remained even in the minds of the loyal angels. Was God the kind of being that Satan had made Him out to be? God could not vindicate Himself by a show of force, but only by a demonstration of His character of love. Our planet became a theatrical stage for the universe (see 1 Cor. 4:9).

God created Adam and Eve as unique beings, in His own image, with the capacity to enter with Him into an intelligent creative process like Himself, through procreation (unlike the angels; see Matt. 22:30). As free moral agents, they received a test to highlight the ultimate essence of morality—to obey God because they loved and trusted Him and not because of any ulterior motives (what they could get out of Him). The Lord placed two trees in the midst of the garden: the tree of life and the tree of knowledge of good and evil. Adam and Eve could freely eat from the tree of life and all the other trees in the garden, but not from the tree of the knowledge of good and evil. The account in Genesis 2 and 3 makes clear that the forbidden tree had

A Song of Redemption

nothing unusual about it that gave Adam and Eve a rational reason to avoid its fruit. Like all of the other trees, it was beautiful and loaded with delicious fruit. And therein lay the test. Would man acquiesce in the joy of obedience in a matter in which God's bidding was the only motivation? It was a small painless test, but Adam and Eve failed, choosing rather to believe the deceptions of a wily serpent creature than the words of their loving Creator.

We have already noted how that in the Garden of Eden before sin, the Sabbath was not really an indicator of loyalty. It was natural for Adam and Eve to want to accept God's invitation for a day of personal fellowship and celebration with Him each week. But after the Fall, when the sinful pair had to leave the garden, they could no longer hold face-to-face communion with their Maker. At that point the Sabbath became a test, like the tree of the knowledge of good and evil had been in the garden.

No longer did God come visibly to meet with them on Sabbaths. The seventh day seemed ostensibly like all the other days. They could see no apparent rational reason for resting from work on the seventh day—except that God had said to do so! The Sabbath thus became a measure of the highest form of morality—to decide, "I will obey, not because of any ulterior motives that I can discover by my reason, but simply because the One who commands is infinitely worthy of my trust and admiration and loyalty."

In the first explicit mention of the Sabbath after the Fall, we find clear evidence that the Sabbath was a unique test of man's obedience to all moral law. Note Exodus 16:4:

> Then the Lord said to Moses, "I will rain down bread from heaven for you. The people are to go out each day and gather enough for that day. In this way I will *test* them and see whether they will follow my instructions [Law, Torah]."

The issue here is clearly not all the commandments of God, but the Sabbath commandment. Yet as the story unfolds and the people of Israel go out to gather manna on the seventh day instead of resting as God had commanded them (verse 27), the Lord asks, "How long do you refuse to keep my *commandments* and my *laws?*" (verse 28, RSV). They broke only one, that regarding the Sabbath, but the words *commandments* and *laws* here are in the *plural*. Is God not attempting to show that the Sabbath is a unique test of obedience to all moral law, a focal point of our morality?

As we move to Exodus 20 and the giving of the law from Mt. Sinai, let us consider the Sabbath commandment more closely in relationship to the other nine in the Decalogue. The other nine commandments make good logical sense to an enlightened conscience. They have a rational explanation that appeals to our native reason. Each simply states general principles of reality, of the proper relationship with God and fellow human beings.

The first commandment says, in effect, worship God *exclusively*. It makes perfect sense if indeed He alone is God. The second commandment tells us to worship God *directly*. Again, if we recognize Him to be a Person capable of direct personal relationships, we would naturally not substitute idols. The third commandment directs us to worship God *reverently* and *sincerely*. Once more, if He is the Creator, the principle of respect for, not trivialization of, His sovereignty is reasonable.

The second table of the Decalogue (the last six commandments) deals with relationships between man and his fellowmen, and they all appeal to our natural reason. We can reduce them to six general moral principles:[15]

5. Respect for one's parents and authority—freedom to receive due honor.

6. Respect for life—freedom from violence.

7. Respect for the integrity of the family—freedom to love.

8. Respect for others' property—the freedom of ownership.

A Song of Redemption

9. Respect for others' reputation—freedom through the truth.

10. Respect for one's soul—freedom from the tyranny of selfishness.

Now, returning to the fourth commandment, we notice that it too contains a reasonable principle: worship God *regularly* and *intimately*. One could even argue that the one-day-in-seven concept is a principle so built into the fabric of reality that we can deduce it through scientific investigation. Many of the structures in nature have a pattern of six completed by a seventh: the geodesic dome shape, the cells of a beehive, the cornea of the eye, many viruses, etc.[16] Some have called the six-seven design "a kind of benchmark of the universe,"[17] and some think it may "prove to be the structure that underlies all of nature."[18] We can easily illustrate its basic pattern by drawing six circles (or you can use coins) of equal size around a central circle of the same size. Each of the six outer circles will touch the central circle and also two of its neighbors. The seventh (central) circle is the key to the design.

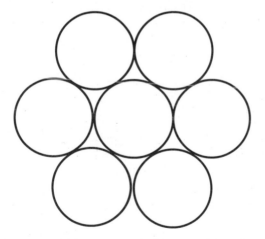

Recent research has revealed examples of a seven-day rhythm in many human physiological functions. The heart rate, the production of steroid hormones, the swelling after surgery, a variety of immune reactions, a higher tendency toward suicide, the rise in the cortical hormones in human mothers' milk—all exhibit "circaseptan biorhythms, or seven-day cycles."[19] Experiments on the optimum work/ rest cycle in Britain during World War II revealed that man produced most efficiently if he worked six days and had one day to rest. In short, we observe mounting evidence for the one-day-in-seven principle. It makes good scientific sense.

But we encounter one point in the Sabbath commandment that is discoverable neither to the enlightened conscience nor to the enterprising scientist: the specific *seventh* day of worship. No amount of native reasoning or scientific investigation will lead one to rest on the seventh day as designated in the Sabbath commandment. The movements of the astronomical bodies regulate the beginning and ending of the daily, monthly, seasonal, and yearly cycles, and we can calculate these with precision. But the seven-day week, ending with the Sabbath, has no relationship to any cyclical changes of nature or movements of heavenly bodies. The seventh-day Sabbath as the climax of the week exists simply because God has declared it so! Thus the Sabbath is the moral nerve center of the law. Far from being the one commandment that is ceremonial and not moral, as some claim, it is a test of the highest morality—to worship God totally, without reservation, because we trust what He says. The Sabbath is the litmus test of what man will do with all moral law. It is the measure of our whole posture toward all of God's expectations. Here is the ultimate test in interpersonal relations.

Since the fourth commandment constitutes a unique indication of human allegiance to God, we should not be surprised that Scripture refers to the Sabbath as a "sign" of the relationship between God and His commandment-keeping people. According to Exodus 31:13, God informs His people Israel, "You must observe my Sabbaths. This will be a sign between me and you for the generations to come, so you may know that I am the Lord, who makes you holy."

A Song of Redemption

Ezekiel gave the same message in his day:

> I gave them my Sabbaths as a sign between us, so they would know that I the Lord made them holy. . . . Keep my Sabbaths holy, that they may be a sign between us. Then you will know that I am the Lord your God (Eze. 20:12, 20).

Both passages have powerful covenantal overtones, and Exodus 31:16, 17 explicitly refers to the celebration of the Sabbath as a sign of the "lasting covenant"—the bond of personal commitment between the people and their God.

This is a phenomenal picture of the wonderful God of Scripture, because no other religion in ancient times had a deity who entered into a covenant with his people. The supposed gods of other nations were capricious and had to be placated. They would use people and coerce them. But the God of the Scriptures is dependable and trustworthy, and He longs to have intimate fellowship with His people. Consequently, He *initiated* the covenant-making process, binding Himself to His people with unfailing covenant love and faithfulness (as we have seen in Psalm 92:1).

The Sabbath is the symbol of His covenant relationship. On the Lord's part, it stands as a guarantee that He will continue to be their God and will make them holy by His intimate presence. On the people's part, it is a sign of loyalty whereby they may demonstrate their allegiance to God by keeping His appointment with them each Sabbath, thus recognizing and acknowledging Him as their Creator and Lord. As Meredith Kline has put it: "The Creator has stamped on world history the sign of the Sabbath as His seal of ownership and authority." [20]

Kline points out that the Sabbath commandment contains the same elements as the ancient suzerain's dynastic seal in the international treaties of Moses' time. Only the fourth commandment has the essential elements of the royal seal: God's identity ("the Lord your God"), God's title (Creator, "the Lord made"), and God's territory ("the heavens and the earth, the sea, and all that is in them"). And the Sabbath commandment appears in the heart of the Decalogue, just as the dynastic seals are often placed in the middle of the ancient treaty documents.[21]

Thus the Sabbath clearly serves as the seal of the Decalogue, the sign of God's commandment-keeping people. If the Sabbath is the special symbol of loyalty to God, we should expect that Satan would make it an object of particular attack. And that is precisely what we find in the biblical record. Already in the years following Israel's exodus from Egypt, God's people began to ignore or profane the Sabbath. God makes this explicit through the prophet Ezekiel:

> Yet the people of Israel rebelled against me in the desert. They did not follow my decrees but rejected my laws—although the man who obeys them will live by them—and they utterly desecrated my Sabbaths (Eze. 20:13).

God emphasizes His charge by repeating the accusation four times in the same chapter (see verses 13, 16, 21, 24).

In Ezekiel's day, just before the Babylonian captivity, Israel again slipped into widespread violation of the Sabbath. What Ezekiel implied, Jeremiah, his contemporary, made plain. The people of Jerusalem worked on the Sabbath in disregard of God's fourth commandment, and Jeremiah had to deliver this stern warning:

> This is what the Lord says: Be careful not to carry a load on the Sabbath day or bring it through the gates of Jerusalem. Do not bring a load out of your houses or do any work on the Sabbath, but keep the Sabbath day holy, as I commanded your forefathers (Jer. 17:21, 22).

In the time of Ezekiel and Jeremiah the people were not only desecrating the Sabbath by working on that day but

A Song of Redemption

they had also turned from the Creator, whose work is memorialized by the Sabbath, to the worship of idols. In vision Ezekiel witnessed various scenes of idolatry in Jerusalem, moving from lesser to greater intensity. But the worst of the abominations was the worship of the sun (see Eze. 8:16-18). The 70-year Babylonian captivity cured Israel of idolatry, but upon their return to Jerusalem, the Jews again failed the test of loyalty in regard to Sabbath-keeping. The prophet Nehemiah was aghast to see the blatant disregard of the Sabbath:

> In those days I saw men in Judah treading wine-presses on the Sabbath and bringing in grain and loading it on donkeys, together with wine, grapes, figs and all other kinds of loads. And they were bringing all this into Jerusalem on the Sabbath (Neh. 13:15).

Realizing the seriousness of such disregard for God's special test of loyalty, Nehemiah took the direct approach:

> I rebuked the nobles of Judah and said to them, 'What is this wicked thing you are doing—desecrating the Sabbath day? Didn't your forefathers do the same things, so that our God brought all this calamity upon us and upon this city? Now you are stirring up more wrath against Israel by desecrating the Sabbath.' When evening shadows fell on the gates of Jerusalem before the Sabbath, I ordered the doors to be shut and not opened until the Sabbath was over. I stationed some of my own men at the gates so that no load could be brought in on the Sabbath day (verses 17-19).

With the reforms of Nehemiah and Ezra, Israel finally learned their lesson regarding the importance of Sabbath observance. But now the enemy of the Sabbath had another device to pervert its true meaning. In intertestamental times

71

the Jews, in their eagerness to carefully guard the sacredness of the Sabbath, began to hedge it about with a multitude of man-made restrictions. The original purpose of the Sabbath as a blessing to man all but vanished under a mass of legalistic rabbinic requirements.

Jesus came and, as we have seen earlier, swept away all the distorted notions and traditions, and restored the Sabbath to its original re-creative and redemptive functions.

We have already noted that the apostles upheld the permanence of the law—including the Sabbath—in its deep spiritual meaning. A host of New Testament passages affirms the continuation of Sabbath observance among the apostles and in the early church, both by Jews and Gentiles (see Matt. 24:20; Acts 13:14, 42-44; 15:19-21; 16:12, 13; 17:1, 2; 18:4; Heb. 4:9; Rev. 1:10; cf. Isa. 58:13; Matt. 12:8). We must emphasize that the early church did not change the seventh-day Sabbath to Sunday. A recent, widely acclaimed polemic against the continuing validity of the seventh-day Sabbath freely acknowledges this fact:

> Again, however, it has been shown that this change of day claim has no biblical evidence to support it. . . . In any case, all the probabilities are against such a change, for the Jewish Sabbath was so distinctive and central to Judaism that any attempts in the early church to tamper with the day on which it was observed would have led to great controversy, and it would be strange indeed that none of the literature of the first and second centuries reflect any such controversy. Further, such a change of day would have caused not only religious but also social and economic turmoil if Jewish Christians had taken their day of rest on a different day and Gentile believers had started to take a day of rest on the first day of every week. Again, of such turmoil there is not a hint.[22]

While the apostles did not alter the Sabbath, they

apparently did have to face certain Judaizers and other heretical syncretistic groups that attempted to burden the Sabbath with man-made restrictions, mandate certain ceremonial fast days, and insist upon the continuation of the ceremonial system of animal sacrifices in connection with the Sabbath. We find glimpses of these and related problems in such passages as Colossians 2:16-23; Galatians 4:8-11; and Romans 14:1-12.[23]

The apostles also warned that a great apostasy would come upon the church, a falling away from crucial Christian doctrines. So writes Paul to the Thessalonians:

> Don't let anyone deceive you in any way, for that day [the second coming of Christ] will not come until the rebellion occurs and the man of lawlessness is revealed, the man doomed to destruction. He opposes and exalts himself over everything that is called God or is worshiped, and even sets himself up in God's temple, proclaiming himself to be God (2 Thess. 2:3, 4).

Paul bears similar witness in Acts 20:29, 30; and 2 Timothy 3:1-5; Peter in 2 Peter 2:1-3; and John in 1 John 4:1-3.

In Old Testament times the prophet Daniel had already seen in prophetic vision the rise of an apostate religious power after the fall of the fourth world empire, Rome. Let me encourage the reader to refer to detailed commentaries, such as C. M. Maxwell's *God Cares: The Message of Daniel for You and Your Family*, for a full exposition of Daniel 7,[24] but note that according to Daniel the "little horn" power would "think to change the times and the law" (verse 25, RSV). There would arise a persecuting religious power that would attempt to tamper with God's law and, in particular, with the aspect of time.

The Protestant Reformers were virtually unanimous in interpreting Daniel 7 as fulfilled in the papal system,[25] and the Roman Church has openly acknowledged that without biblical support it has changed the part of the law dealing with time—the Sabbath commandment.

As I write these words, I have before me my copy of *The Question Box Answers: Replies to Questions Received on Missions to Non-Catholics,* by Rev. Bertrand L. Conway, of the Paulist Fathers, with a preface by Cardinal Gibbons. On page 179 appear the questions:

> What Bible authority is there for changing the Sabbath from the seventh to the first day of the week? Who gave the pope the authority to change a command of God?

Here is Conway's reply:

> If the Bible is the only guide for the Christian, then the Seventh-day Adventist is right in observing Saturday with the Jew. . . . Is it not strange that those who make the Bible their only teacher should inconsistently follow in this matter the tradition of the church?

Cardinal Gibbons himself writes in his *Faith of our Fathers* (92nd ed., p. 89):

> You may read the Bible from Genesis to Revelation, and you will not find a single line authorizing the sanctification of Sunday. The Scriptures enforce the religious observance of Saturday, a day which we never sanctify.

The acknowledgment of the change of the Sabbath could not be more explicit than in *The Convert's Catechism of Catholic Doctrine*:

Q. Which is the Sabbath day?
A. Saturday is the Sabbath day.
Q. Why do we observe Sunday instead of Saturday?
A. We observe Sunday instead of Saturday because

A Song of Redemption

the Catholic Church in the Council of Laodicea (A.D.
336) transferred the solemnity from Saturday to
Sunday.[26]

The displacement of the seventh-day Sabbath by Sunday
involved a long, slow process. The full story of how Christianity effected the change from Sabbath to Sunday is a
fascinating one, and would require a separate volume to
relate in detail.[27] But in brief, early in the second century
A.D. Roman anti-Judaism had already come to a head.
Christians, particularly in the capital city of Rome and in the
cultural center of Alexandria, sought to distance themselves
from any identification with Jewish practices, including the
seventh-day Sabbath. In place of the "Jewish" Sabbath, an
annual celebration of Easter evolved into a weekly Christian
Sunday.

Outside of Rome and Alexandria large segments of the
church observed both Sunday and Sabbath at the same time
for centuries. Even as late as the fifth century, church
historians Socrates Scholasticus and Sozomon described
the situation as follows:

> For although almost all churches throughout the
> world celebrate the sacred mysteries [the Lord's Sup-
> per] on the Sabbath [Saturday] of every week, yet the
> Christians of Alexandria and at Rome, on account of
> some ancient tradition, have ceased to do this.[28]

> The people of Constantinople, and almost every-
> where, assemble together on the Sabbath, as well as
> on the first day of the week, which custom is never
> observed at Rome or at Alexandria.[29]

For a time many still regarded the Sabbath as the
divinely commanded day of rest and worship, while Sunday
was only a day of religious services and recreation. But
gradually throughout the empire anti-Jewish sentiments
encouraged church leaders to transform the Sabbath into a

day of somber fasting, in contrast to the Jews, who never fasted on Sabbath. Sunday, on the other hand, continued to be a joyous festival, and gained even more popular favor because it coincided in time with the weekly pagan festival held on the "venerable day of the sun." Eventually the pagan emperor Constantine converted to Christianity, and "the gods of popularity and compromise" prevailed over the Bible Sabbath. As William Frederick puts it:

> At this time it was necessary for the church to either adopt the Gentiles' day or else have the Gentiles change their day. To change the Gentiles' day would have been an offense and a stumbling block to them. The church could naturally reach them better by keeping their day.[30]

In a momentous enactment on March 7, 321, Emperor Constantine wedded paganism with Christianity by elevating "the venerable day of the sun" to the status of a civil rest day throughout the empire.[31] With Sunday now firmly in place as a rest day, a second rest day on Sabbath could not last long. And that brings us to the first Catholic Church council to deal with Sunday as a day of rest: the Council of Laodicea (A.D. 364). Canon 29 of that council reads:

> Christians shall not Judaize and be idle on Saturday but shall work on that day; but the Lord's day they shall especially honor, and, as being Christians, shall, if possible, do no work on that day. If, however, they are found Judaizing, they shall be shut out from Christ.[32]

The council's historic decision formally transferred the sanctity of the seventh-day Sabbath to Sunday and legislated Saturday as a workday. Later official church pronouncements solidified and intensified this landmark canon law:

A Song of Redemption

In nearly every council the Sabbath which God had instituted was pressed down a little lower, while the Sunday was correspondingly exalted. Thus the pagan festival came finally to be honored as a divine institution, while the Bible Sabbath was pronounced a relic of Judaism, and its observers were declared to be accursed. The great apostate had succeeded in exalting himself "above all that is called God, or that is worshiped" (2 Thess. 2:4). He had dared to change the only precept of the divine law that unmistakably points all mankind to the true and living God.[33]

Although throughout the Christian era some have always been faithful seventh-day Sabbathkeepers,[34] their numbers have been few. Sunday has triumphed in Christendom.

Most Christians do not realize the origin of Sunday observance, and thus almost the whole Christian world today accepts it as their day of worship. Certainly God does not hold sincere Christians responsible for light they have not yet received, but "the path of the righteous is like the first gleam of dawn, shining ever brighter till the full light of day" (Prov. 4:18). Since the time of the Reformation, many vital teachings have once more emerged from the darkness of pagan-Christian apostasy.[35] And before Christ returns again, He has still another special truth that needs to shine forth again in all its brilliance. The Sabbath song, barely audible through so many centuries, needs once more to swell into a mighty chorus!

The Sabbath concept lies at the heart of the three angels' messages, recorded in Revelation 14. This chapter begins with a description of the final generation of God's redeemed, who have "his name [character] . . . written on their foreheads [minds]" (verses 1-5), and it ends with a description of Christ's second coming (verses 14-20). In the heart of the chapter (verses 6-13) we find the awesome threefold warning to prepare the world for Christ's coming, to prepare a pure and holy people such as were described in verses 1-5. Note in particular the message of the first angel:

A LOVE SONG FOR THE SABBATH

> Then I saw another angel flying in midair, and he had
> the eternal gospel to proclaim to those who live on
> the earth—to every nation, tribe, language and peo-
> ple. He said in a loud voice, "Fear God and give him
> glory, because the hour of his judgment has come.
> Worship him who made the heavens, the earth, the
> sea and the springs of water" (Rev. 14:6, 7).

As part of the final judgment-hour message, we find a
call to worship God. And what will constitute such faithful
worship? Notice that in the last part of his appeal, the angel
cites part of the fourth commandment. He points to God,
"who made the heavens, the earth, the sea and the springs
of water." Here again is the *seal* of God, which we encoun-
tered in the fourth commandment: His name ("God"), His
authority ("the Creator"), and His territory ("the heavens and
the earth"). The revival of the worship of the Creator
includes the restoration of the seal of His law, the Sabbath,
as an acknowledgment of His authority.

God's last-day people will include a remnant who obey
all of His commandments, including the fourth. An emphasis upon obedience to all of God's law appears in the
conclusion of the third angel's message: "Here is a call for
the endurance of the saints, those who keep the commandments of God and the faith of Jesus" (Rev. 14:12, RSV). We
have already seen that the law of the New Testament is the
same as the Decalogue in the Old Testament. John's vision
in Revelation 11:19 of the heavenly sanctuary, the original
after which the earthly was copied, confirms this.[36] The
revelator sees that in the last days the inner apartment of
the heavenly sanctuary will open to reveal the "ark of his
covenant," which contains the "tablets of the covenant," the
Ten Commandments (cf. Deut. 9:9-12; Deut. 10:1-5).

Inasmuch as the same law is in force during John's time,
we should expect that the Sabbath commandment would
continue to be a special sign of loyalty to God. Isaiah had
written, "Seal up the law among my disciples" (Isa. 8:16).
The Sabbath, as we have seen, is the seal of the law. It is the

one commandment that humanity contests, the one commandment not discernable by native reason but that de-
pends wholly upon our recognition of God as Creator and
our willingness to do what He says for His sake alone. Truly
it is the commandment in which the "faith of Jesus"—
implicit trust in God's word, as Jesus did—comes most
intensely into focus.

In the last days God will have a people, a "remnant" (Rev.
12:17, KJV), who trust Him without reservation. A people
who are willing to do what their trustworthy God says
simply because He has said so. A people who will worship
Him by restoring the seal of His creatorship. A people who
are willing to obey His commandments, including the
fourth, which nearly all the world opposes.

And all the world *will* resist such obedience. Revelation
13 brings into view the same apostate religious power that
was described in Daniel 7 (see especially the parallels in
Revelation 13:5), the power that would tamper with God's
law.[37] Just as God has His special seal, or sign of loyalty, in
the Sabbath, so according to Revelation 13:16, 17, the false
religious system has a counterfeit sign, or mark, which
Daniel 7 shows to be the change in the "time" of the law—
the substitution of a counterfeit day of worship. We have
already seen examples of the kind of reasoning this claim
will take:

> The observance of Sunday by the Protestants is an
> homage they pay, in spite of themselves, to the
> authority of the [Catholic] Church.[38]

> Question: How prove you that the church hath power
> to command feasts and holy days?
> Answer: By the very act of changing the Sabbath into
> Sunday, which Protestants allow of, and therefore
> they fondly contradict themselves by keeping Sunday
> strictly, and breaking most other feasts commanded
> by the same church.
> Question: How prove you that?

Answer: Because by keeping Sunday they acknowl-edge the church's power to ordain feasts and to command them under sin.[39]

Of course the Catholic Church claims that the change was her act. . . And the act is a *mark* of her ecclesiastical authority in religious things.[40]

Revelation 13 warns that an apostate religious system will at the end of time seek to coerce mankind into acceptance of a special mark of authority. The system will employ economic boycott and eventually a death decree for those who refuse to accept the beast's false day of worship (see Rev. 13:15, 16).

During this time of crisis, the issues will become plain to all. The solemn messages of the second and third angels of Revelation 14 will go forth to the world, warning of the false doctrines of spiritual Babylon and urging the inhabitants of the earth not to worship the beast nor to accept his distinguishing mark of loyalty. They will swell into the loud cry of Revelation 18:1-3. God's people will proclaim the Sabbath more fully. All will have opportunity to see that it is not just a matter of one day versus another, but that it involves the highest test of moral integrity. Will humanity serve God and obey Him simply because He asks them to, even when it goes against their feelings and perceptions? Will they be loyal to God even when they see no apparent advantage for doing so, and every apparent disadvantage?

The crisis at the close of earth's history centers on the same issue as at mankind's beginning in the Garden of Eden. Two trees in the garden—to all external appearances they looked alike. Why eat of one and not of the other? Not because of any intrinsic evidence discernable to human reason or research, but because God declared it so. Two days of the week—to all external appearances they seem alike. Why worship on one and not another? Not because of any intrinsic property of holiness that native reason or the enlightened conscience can recognize, but because God

A Song of Redemption

blessed and sanctified one and not the other.

At the end of time the whole world will have to face this most basic test of moral issues. Their decision will reveal their ultimate loyalties. Those who have become so settled in their commitment to God that nothing can shake them from loyalty to Him—they would rather die than disregard God's seal, the Sabbath—will have that seal indelibly impressed upon their minds ("foreheads," Rev. 7:2-8;14:1). They are God's special possession—eternally secure and safe to save (see Rev. 7). And those who have seen clearly the light of the Sabbath message but have chosen to accept the counterfeit sign of loyalty to the enemy of God—his day of worship—will finally become unalterably locked into rebellion against God and receive the mark of allegiance to the beast (see Rev. 13:16, 17). Their choice has become so deeply imbedded into their habit patterns and personalities that it is irreversible. Probation is closed. Nothing remains but the plagues, the final judgment, and the lake of fire (see Rev. 15-20).

You may be wondering what such somber scenes can possibly have to do with a love song of redemption. Have we not strayed far from Psalm 92? No indeed! We have actually filled in the details from the rest of Scripture for the last lines of the Sabbath redemption stanza (verse 9): "For surely your enemies, O Lord, surely your enemies will perish; all evildoers will be scattered."

And Psalm 92:9 is nothing less than the echo of the greatest song of redemption in the history of the universe. As verse 7 points backward to the Song of Moses and the *past* redemption of Israel from Egyptian bondage so verse 9 directs us forward to the ultimate *future* redemption song—the Song of Moses and the Lamb. John the revelator in vision saw the singers and heard the song.

> And I saw what looked like a sea of glass mixed with fire and, standing beside the sea, those who had been victorious over the beast and his image and over the number of his name. They held harps given them

A LOVE SONG FOR THE SABBATH

by God and sang the song of Moses the servant of God and the song of the Lamb: "Great and marvelous are your deeds, Lord God Almighty. Just and true are your ways, King of the ages. Who will not fear you, O Lord, and bring glory to your name? For you alone are holy. All nations will come and worship before you, for your righteous acts have been revealed" (Rev. 15:2-4).

What a song of glorious triumph!

Redemption and the Character of God

Thus far it has become apparent in our discussion, and is highlighted again in the Song of Moses and the Lamb, that the *ultimate question* in the struggle between good and evil concerns the *character* of God. Is He the Lord, the covenant-making God who comes to fellowship with His people, and, at the same time, the Almighty—the infinite God? Is He all powerful and all-loving? Are His ways just and true? Are His deeds great and marvelous? Is He alone holy, worthy of our worship? The issue of God's character leads us to the heart of Psalm 92, to the central verse containing the core message of the Sabbath: "But you, O Lord, are exalted forever" (verse 8).

Everything hinges upon our views of the character of God. Is He our Lord, *Yahweh,* our personal covenant God? Is He also the infinite, exalted One in our lives? Are we willing to do what He says because we trust Him, because we have absolute confidence in Him? Are we willing to give Him the place of exaltation that He deserves?

In the very opening stanza of the Sabbath love song we found the character of God emphasized. "It is good to . . . make music to your name [or character]," sings the psalmist. "To proclaim your love in the morning and your faithfulness at night," he continues (verses 1, 2). God's character is also the burden of the final stanza of the song,

A Song of Redemption

which concludes with the proclamation "The Lord is upright; he is my Rock, and there is no wickedness in him" (verse 15).

As we have already seen, the conflict between God and Satan began in heaven as Lucifer questioned God's character. Our world became a theater for the universe, as God presented His newly created man and woman with an opportunity to reveal to the heavenly intelligences that He was not the kind of being that Satan had charged. The drama playing on our world would demonstrate that He was infinitely worthy of His creatures' love and devotion, not for anything they could get out of Him, but for His own sake. By means of a simple test, Adam and Eve, as free moral agents, would have an opportunity to reveal their loyalty and devotion to their Creator. In the garden the crucial issue centered on the question Who will you trust? The two trees looked equally desirable, but God commanded them to eat of one and abstain from the other. The Lord had already given abundant evidence of His trustworthiness in all the wonderful works He had made for their happiness and by His loving fellowship with Adam and Eve at the tree of life, particularly on Sabbath. But as Eve thoughtlessly separated from her husband and wandered near the forbidden tree, the serpent from its branches called into question God's character and motives, and produced his counterfeit evidence. Had not the serpent's eating of the forbidden fruit given him the power of speech? Just think what it would do for Adam and Eve—they would become like God!

And so she, and later Adam, found themselves brought to a choice—the highest test of their moral integrity. Would they trust God and do what He said, even when their senses, dazzled by the serpent, betrayed them and the deceiver pressed them to disobey?

With the Sabbath the issue is the same. God blessed and sanctified (or set aside) the seventh day. Since the Fall, and particularly now at the end of time, God's holy day has become a sign of loyalty to Him. And today, as always, the basic question is Can God be trusted? The Sabbath looks exactly like the other days of the week. On it we breathe no fresher air nor observe brighter sunshine. But God has given ample evidence of His love and faithfulness, available particularly in the fellowship of the Sabbath. Humanity must decide not just on a matter of one day or another, but on this ultimate question: Is God the kind of God He claims to be, infinitely worthy of our loyalty and worship for His own sake? We must decide whether or not to be faithful to Him in the highest form of moral test—whether to trust what He says regarding a commandment for which we have no intrinsic evidence or reason except the command itself. Doing so is the sign of total surrender to His will. In the final generation, by choosing such loyalty, God's people will have the opportunity to give a mass witness to the universe that He indeed is worthy of unreserved trust. The final victory song of the saints will be: "Just and true are your ways, King of the ages" (Rev. 15:4). Then the whole universe, before which God stands fully vindicated, will take up the hallelujah strain: "Salvation and glory and power belong to our God, for true and just are his judgments" (Rev. 19:1, 2).

The song of redemption has reached its grand climax.

When as the grass the wicked did grow,
When sinners flourished here below,
Then was there endless ruin nigh,
But Thou, O Lord, art throned on high;
Thy foes shall fall before Thy might,
The wicked shall be put to flight (Ps. 92:7-9, paraphrased).

References

[1] See Delitzsch, *Commentary on the Old Testament: Psalms,* vol. 3, p. 65; Nahum M. Sarna, "The Psalm for the Sabbath Day [Ps. 92]," *Journal of Biblical Literature* 81 (1962): 159.

[2] See E. J. Kissane, *The Book of Psalms* (Dublin: Brown and Nolan, 1964), vol. 2, pp. 110, 112.

[3] Ellen G. White, *Education* (Mountain View, Calif.: Pacific Press Pub. Assn., 1952), p. 162.

[4] See Hasel, "The Sabbath in the Pentateuch," in Strand, *The Sabbath in*

A Song of Redemption

Scripture and History, pp. 31-33; Niels-Erik Andreasen, *Rest and Redemption: A Study of the Biblical Sabbath* (Berrien Springs, Mich.: Andrews University Press, 1978), pp. 48-53.

[5] See especially Samuele Bacchiocchi, *The Sabbath in the New Testament* (Berrien Springs, Mich.: Biblical Perspectives, 1985), pp. 66-79; and John Brunt, *A Day for Healing: The Meaning of Jesus' Sabbath Miracles* (Washington, D.C.: Review and Herald Pub. Assn., 1981), pp. 19-43.

[6] Stott, "Sabbath," in Brown, *The New International Dictionary of New Testament Theology,* vol. 3, p. 409.

[7] *Ibid.*

[8] *Ibid.,* p. 410.

[9] See Brunt, pp. 44-54, for an elaboration of the ideas in this paragraph.

[10] See Bacchiocchi, pp. 71, 72.

[11] Samuele Bacchiocchi, "A Memorial of Redemption," in Roy Branson, ed., *Festival of the Sabbath* (Takoma Park, Md.: Association of Adventist Forums, 1985), p. 62. As Jesus so clearly said: "You will find rest for your *souls*" (Matt. 11:29).

[12] Note the contrast with the sacrificial system, which did become obsolete with the coming of Christ; the apostle forcefully points out its self-confessed obsolescence (see Heb. 10:1-10).

[13] Ellen White Comments, *The SDA Bible Commentary,* cf. Ellen G. White, *Thoughts From the Mount of Blessing* (Mountain View, Calif.: Pacific Press Pub. Assn., 1943), p. 1.

[14] See Isa. 14; Eze. 28; Rev. 12; and the biblical summary in Ellen G. White, *The Great Controversy* (Mountain View, Calif.: Pacific Press Pub. Assn., 1950), pp. 492-504.

[15] See the discussion in James Londis, *God's Finger Wrote Freedom* (Washington, D.C.: Review and Herald Pub. Assn., 1978), pp. 39-116.

[16] See *Time,* Jan. 10, 1964, pp. 46-51.

[17] *Ibid.*

[18] *Reader's Digest,* Nov. 1969, p. 206.

[19] See Bernell Baldwin, "Seven-Day Rhythms," *Journal of Health and Healing* 9 (1984): 3, 14. Baldwin cites a number of impressive scientific studies supporting this conclusion.

[20] Kline, *Treaty of the Great King,* p. 19.

[21] *Ibid.,* pp. 18, 19.

[22] A. T. Lincoln, "From Sabbath to Lord's Day: A Biblical and Theological Perspective," in D. A. Carson, ed., *From Sabbath to Lord's Day: A Biblical, Historical, and Theological Investigation* (Grand Rapids: Mich.: Zondervan, 1982), p. 393. The New Testament passages mentioning the first day of the week (Sunday) clearly do not ascribe any holiness to that day or give any hint of Sunday observance replacing the Sabbath. For discussion, see Walter Specht, "Sunday in the New Testament," in Strand, pp. 114-129.

[23] On Col. 2, see especially Paul Giem, "Sabbaton in Col. 2:16," *Andrews University Seminary Studies* 19 (1981): 195-210; On Rom. 14 (and Gal. 4), see especially Raoul Dederen, "On Esteeming One Day Better Than Another," *Andrews University Seminary Studies* 9 (1971): 16-35, abbreviated as Appendix C in Strand, pp. 333-337.

[24] C. Mervyn Maxwell, *God Cares. The Message of Daniel for You and Your Family* (Mountain View, Calif.: Pacific Press Pub. Assn., 1981), pp. 101-143.

[25] See LeRoy Edwin Froom, *The Prophetic Faith of Our Fathers* (Washington,

D.C.: Review and Herald Pub. Assn., 1948), vol. 2, especially pp. 528-532 (summary charts).

[26] *Ibid.*, 2nd ed., 1910, p. 50. The 1977 edition is identical except for the omission of the reference to the Council of Laodicea.

[27] See especially Samuele Bacchiocchi, *From Sabbath to Sunday: A Historical Investigation of the Rise of Sunday Observance in Early Christianity* (Rome: The Pontifical Gregorian University Press, 1977); cf. the summary in S. Bacchiocchi, "The Rise of Sunday Observance in Early Christianity," in Strand, pp. 132-150. Bacchiocchi's treatment of the rise of Sunday, particularly in Rome, is augmented by the broader analysis of Kenneth A. Strand's "The Sabbath and Sunday From the Second Through Fifth Centuries," in Strand, pp. 323-332.

[28] Socrates Scholasticus, *Ecclesiastical History* 5. 22, cited in Strand, p. 323.

[29] Sozoman *Ecclesiastical History* 7. 19 (NPNF/2 2:390), cited in Strand, p. 324.

[30] William Frederick, *Three Prophetic Days*, pp. 169, 170, cited in George Vandeman, *A Day to Remember* (Mountain View, Calif.: Pacific Press Pub. Assn., 1965), p. 62.

[31] *Codex Justinianus* 3.12.3, cited in Strand, p. 328.

[32] Charles J. Hefele, *A History of the Councils of the Church*, vol. 2, p. 316, cited in Strang, p. 329.

[33] White, *The Great Controversy*, pp. 53, 54.

[34] *Ibid.*, p. 61. See Strand, pp. 151-263, for documentation.

[35] For an overview of these developments, see White, *The Great Controversy*, pp. 120-581.

[36] Heb. 8:5; 9:24. See Richard M. Davidson, *Typology in Scripture* (Berrien Springs, Mich.: Andrews University Press, 1981), pp. 336-388.

[37] For a discussion of the striking parallels between Dan. 7 and Rev. 13, and for fuller treatment of the points that follow in this chapter, see C. Mervyn Maxwell, *God Cares, The Message of Revelation for You and Your Family* (Boise: Pacific Press Pub. Assn., 1985), pp. 324-331; 375-386; White, *The Great Controversy*, pp. 433-450.

[38] Louis G. Segure, *Plain Talk About the Protestantism of Today* (Boston: Thomas B. Noonan, 1868), p. 213.

[39] *Douay Catechism*, p. 59.

[40] H. F. Thomas, chancellor of Cardinal Gibbons.

Chapter 5

A Song of Sanctification

You have exalted my horn like that of a wild ox;
fine oils have been poured upon me.
My eyes have seen the defeat of my adversaries;
my ears have heard the rout of my wicked foes.
The righteous will flourish like a palm tree,
they will grow like a cedar of Lebanon.
—Ps. 92:10-12

In previous stanzas of our Sabbath Psalm we have sung of several powerful motivations for Sabbath joy—Creation and redemption in the past and final redemption in the future. Based upon this foundation—the awareness of our creatureliness and our assurance of redemption—we may go on to ever-spiraling heights of attainment and joy. The fourth stanza of the Sabbath love song (verses 10-12) brings us to the here and now: we sing of our present experience as epitomized by the Sabbath.

The Abundant Life

Images of the abundant life come fast and glorious in this stanza. As you sing, absorb their wondrous message! The exalted horn—rejoice in this biblical symbol of defensive and offensive power and victory in the Christian life. Let it sink in—*God* does the exalting; He takes responsibility for your success. The wild ox (or ibex)—picture your God-given freedom from all tyranny of time and schedule. Assimilate the divine promise in the psalmist's striking imagery—poise and gracefulness like the ibex bounding over the mountaintops. Experience the calmness that fills the life of the person who knows the Lord of the Sabbath. As you cling to the strength of such a God, no amount of trouble or turmoil can destroy you.

The fine oil—feel the soothing and healing balm poured upon your wounds in life. Sense the refreshing of the Spirit as He energizes and fills you with enthusiasm. The defeat of your adversaries—taste the joy of *present* victory over spiritual foes, as well as past deliverance and future assurance of conquest.

Experience the growth, the flourishing, not like the grass that soon withers, but like the date palm—called by the inhabitants of the Near East a "blessed tree, the sister of man." See its perennial green foliage, its vital force constantly renewing itself from its roots. Its diadem of leaves—grasp the symbol of your victory and royalty in Christ. Behold its fruit, more than 600 pounds of yield in a single season. Bask in the usefulness and productivity God promises for your future.

Gaze at the mighty cedar of Lebanon—prince among the trees of the mountains, graceful, with lofty growth. Sense its year-round greenness and the pleasant perfume of its needles, and visualize the freshness and fragrance of life that is yours. Claim the promised strength and nobility symbolized by the cedar of Lebanon.

In short, this section of Psalm 92 tells us to absorb the meaning of the Sabbath; it is a promise of the abundant and victorious life. Thus it is the sign of sanctification. The song of Psalm 92 is the melodic counterpart of Exodus 31:13: "You shall keep my sabbaths, for this is a sign between me and you throughout your generations, that you may know that I, the Lord, sanctify you" (RSV). Just as the Lord rested on the seventh day after creating the earth and was "refreshed," or literally, "took on new life" (verse 17, RSV), so He offers us the gifts of this same life, ever new. "The Sabbath is a sign of Christ's power to make us holy."[1] The Sabbath, that "golden clasp"[2] that binds us to our Maker

A Song of Sanctification

and Redeemer, links us also to our Sanctifier. With the Sabbath comes the promise: You may have the highest expectations and loftiest aspirations. In the power of the Spirit there will be no limit to your usefulness. Flourish as the date palm. Let your watchword be *excelsior!* ("higher!") or better, *excelissimus!* ("the highest!"). Through the grace of Him who sanctifies you, you may turn the desert of your life into a palm-treed oasis. You may stand nobly, cedars upon the mountaintops!

The Sanctification of the Sabbath

How does the sanctification of the Sabbath come about? Is there some magical quality about the day that automatically transmits holiness, or sanctification? Obviously not. Rather, as we have already seen, Sabbath is the day God has set aside for special fellowship with His creatures on earth. God makes the day holy, or sacred, by gracing it with His presence. And therefore the Sabbath does not "stand simply for holiness of time or holy time, but holiness in time, or holy people."[3]

By communing with God, we actually partake of His holiness. Thus because its hours are filled with intimate fellowship between man and God, the Sabbath becomes the sign, the epitome, of the entire life of sanctification.

God has placed a glorious opportunity and privilege before us. In a special way on Sabbath we may put aside our daily work and participate in deep personal communion with the Holy One of Israel, and in that intimate relationship become changed more and more into His likeness.

God longs to make us holy through His presence with us on His holy Sabbath day. He knows that this sanctifying personal relationship is vital to our spiritual growth and development. It is because of humanity's desperate need of Sabbath holiness that God imposed such harsh penalties in Old Testament times for disregarding the Sabbath (see Ex. 31:14). He knew that if man desecrated it—that is, treated it as a common day—he could not receive the blessing of sanctification promised during its hours. In essence, man would miss out on the Lord's one great purpose for man—to make him holy. Thus God provided as drastic a deterrent as possible to keep humanity from losing the Sabbath blessing of sanctification. He called for a reform in Sabbath observance in Isaiah's day, in Nehemiah's day, and again in the earthly ministry of Jesus.

And today He summons modern man, who in our age of creeping secularism has lost so much of the sense of the sacred, to recapture the deep spiritual meaning and experience of Sabbath holiness.

Sabbath Reformation

God never appeals to us to reform without showing the way. To our materialistic, secularistic society the message of Sabbath restoration in the book of Isaiah has particular relevance. Already in Isaiah 56 the prophet portrays the Sabbath revival that will take place during the last days:

Maintain justice and do what is right,
>   for my salvation is close at hand,
>   and my righteousness will soon be revealed.

Blessed is the man who does this,
>   the man who holds it fast,
> who keeps the Sabbath without desecrating it,
>   and keeps his hand from doing any evil. . . .

Foreigners who bind themselves to the Lord to serve
>   him, to love the name of the Lord,
>   and to worship him,
> all who keep the Sabbath without desecrating it
>   and who hold fast to my covenant—

these I will bring to my holy mountain
>   and give them joy in my house of prayer
>   (verses 1-7).

A Song of Sanctification

That the passage applies to the Christian age is apparent from the allusion to the gathering of the Gentiles in verse 8:

I will gather still others to them
besides those already gathered.

The appeal for Sabbath reform begun in Isaiah 56 reaches a climax in Isaiah 58. It is crucial to note that the larger context of Isaiah 58 is the occasion of *Yom Kippur,* or Day of Atonement, the day of cleansing and judgment at the close of Israel's religious year. Numerous allusions to the Day of Atonement appear throughout the chapter.[4] Based upon evidence from Scripture, we believe that we are in the last days of the present world's history—we are living in the antitypical day of atonement[5]—and thus Isaiah's message of Sabbath restoration applies with particular force to our generation. It is a call to repentance and reformation in view of imminent judgment. God longs to have a people whom He can describe as the spiritual "repairer of the breach, the restorer of streets to dwell in" (Isa. 58:12, RSV). The fact that the phrases occur immediately before explicit instruction regarding Sabbath reform (verses 13, 14) seems to imply that the proclamation of the Sabbath message will heal a breach—a breach in God's law—and that Sabbath revival will accomplish a spiritual restoration.

The call of Isaiah 58 is not simply a call to return to a correct day; it is a call to recapture the meaning of Sabbath sanctification. This chapter provides a guide for modern man in a secular age on how to "remember the Sabbath day, to keep it holy" (Ex. 20:8, KJV), how to encounter the Holy One of Israel on His holy day.

We may translate Isaiah 58:13, 14 literally in this way:

If you turn your foot away from the Sabbath,
from doing your business [or "whatever you please"] on
My holy day,

and call the Sabbath an exquisite delight,
    the holy of the Lord, honorable,
if you honor it [or "Him"] by not doing
    your [own] ways,
    by not seeking after your [own] business
    [or "whatever you please"],
    or speaking [your own] words,
then you shall find exquisite delight
    in the Lord,
    and I will cause you to ride on the
    heights of the earth;
and I will feed you with the heritage of
    Jacob your father,
    for the mouth of the Lord has spoken.

The first clause asks the reader to "turn his foot away from the Sabbath." A parallel experience came to Moses when he approached the burning bush, and God told him, "Do not come any closer. . . . Take off your sandals, for the place where you are standing is holy ground" (Ex. 3:5). The Sabbath is "holy ground," or rather, holy time. Like Moses, we need to heed the call to remove our spiritual shoes from before our holy God. On Sabbath we enter into His palace— a palace in time. We turn away our feet from business as usual, from that which is common. Only then do we "cease to tread the sabbath underfoot" (Isa. 58:13, NEB). As a result, we do not take it to ourselves to do with as we please.

A Day of Exquisite Delight

Is this a restriction? Never! We must understand this seemingly negative prohibition in light of the positive affirmation in the next phrase: "and call the Sabbath a delight." The word *oneg* ("delight") means literally "exquisite delight," and in its only other Old Testament occurrence as a noun describes the palaces of royalty. In truth, on Sabbath we have an appointment with the King of kings! Picture it: He is coming to honor us with His presence for a

A Song of Sanctification

whole day each week, or if you prefer, He has invited us to His palace for an all-day spiritual feast and fellowship. Then add another brush stroke: this royal Personage has also chosen us as His lover, to be His bride. He invites us for intimate fellowship—an all-day date with the King. In the face of such glorious prospects, who would consider it an unwelcome restriction to drop his "business as usual"?

I have not always understood the Sabbath in such a way. For many years I thought the phrase "not . . . seeking your own pleasure" (verse 13, RSV) meant that the Sabbath could not be a day of real joy and delight. Somehow I had not absorbed the significance of the next phrase "and call the Sabbath a delight." I did not know that the Hebrew for the phrase "seeking your own pleasure" is more appropriately rendered in modern English more as "doing as you please" (NIV), or in light of its usage in Isaiah 58:3 (margin), "pursuing your own business" (RSV). God does not prohibit pleasure on Sabbath—rather, He is calling us to the highest pleasure, that which pleases and satisfies because of its delicate beauty and regal charm.

An understanding of the Sabbath as exquisite delight has revolutionized the Sabbathkeeping in our family. What I describe in the next paragraphs is the ideal to which we aspire and in which we rejoice, though we do not always attain it as we would like.

We try to set the mood each week by reminding each other that on Friday night, royalty is our guest. That calls for flowers on the table, for candlelight, for the best china and dinnerware. The first Friday evening that my wife, Jo Ann, set out our wedding china, my little girl asked, "Who's coming for dinner?" Jo Ann answered exuberantly, "The King is coming!" and little Rahel's eyes shone with delight. Until then we had hesitated to use our best dishes for our children for fear of breakage; but throwing caution to the wind, we put them out, and not one has been broken yet. Too many dishes to wash on Sabbath, you say? We just rinse them off and leave them for the "household servants" to do after Sabbath. For you see, on Sabbath we consider ourselves kings and queens (see 1 Peter 2:9) dining with the King of kings in royal banquet. Only after sunset Saturday night do we return to being domestic help.

Earlier in this book I described some of the family mealtime customs that we have adopted to make Friday evening an occasion of exquisite delight. The Sabbath flowers and Sabbath toast to the King, the special delicious Sabbath bread, the table hymns and candlelight—all give a festive aura to our Sabbath celebration. Some of our other sundown worship traditions I have also mentioned include: the queen of the house lighting Sabbath candles and her fervent prayer for the sanctification of the Sabbath; the father's song to his beloved wife (Prov. 31) and his blessing of his children as he hugs them tightly in his arms.

Before our Sabbath worship, I unplug the phone—a visible signal that what we are doing is the most important thing in the world. Nothing will interrupt our audience with the King. As our call to sundown worship I play on the piano "Day Is Dying in the West." Then I stir the imagination of our children with a mighty blast on a ram's horn—to announce the arrival of the Sabbath as it was done in Jesus' day. With staccato strumming of the guitar in a minor key, I simulate the thunder tones of Mount Sinai, and in solemn grandeur, we repeat the words of God, the fourth commandment. Jo Ann leads us in rousing Sabbath songs of joy punctuated by our children's favorite choices, and culminating in "Dear Lord and Father" *(The SDA Hymnal,* No. 481). In a sharing time we express ways we have been special to each other during the past week. Then we kneel and hold each other close for our Sabbath prayer, the blessing of the children, and the Lord's prayer. We close our formal worship time with "Shalom" *(The SDA Hymnal,* No. 674) and a hearty: "Shabbat shalom!" ("Sabbath peace!").

The rest of Friday evening we reserve especially for our children. Sometimes the kids and I plan and perform Bible charades for Mommy to guess. Sometimes we read animal stories or look at slides of adventures in nature that we have taken. Other times the children put on a sacred concert.

A Song of Sanctification

Before bedtime we try to have a half hour of special time—Mom with daughter, Dad with son (and vice versa every other week)—to read Bible stories, play Bible games, sing hymns a cappella from the new *SDA Hymnal,* or just rub each other's back and talk. After the children are tucked in bed, Jo Ann plays her favorite hymns softly on the piano till they are asleep. Then my beloved and I often continue singing around the piano, curl up with the *Adventist Review* or other devotional reading, or spend some time together in intimate fellowship and dialogue. What a glorious day the Sabbath is! What an exquisite delight!

The joy continues on Sabbath morning. We rise early so the children can eat breakfast to the accompaniment of the children's story on our local Adventist radio station. Sabbath is the day for the special clothes that we save for this time of wondrous fellowship with the King.[6] Our family likes to go to first church service so we can sit on the front pew and Rahel and Jonathan can enjoy the children's story. It is our good fortune to have a pastor whose sermons feed the whole family, including the children. The music also is special, particularly the hymns. Frequently Jo Ann calls the church office early in the week to find out what hymns will be used and plays and sings them at the piano all week to make them more familiar. Then invariably at church one of the children will whisper as the organist begins, "Mommy, Daddy, I know this hymn." By this method (and subsequent review) the children have already learned the words to more hymns than I have.

Sabbath school is the high point of the week for our children. Our congregation has excellent teachers, full of creative ideas and bubbling over with enthusiasm, who put together programs that involve the children and catch their interest. There is no "you'd better be good or Jesus won't love you" spirit, but rather a love and acceptance of the gospel that is irresistible.

We try to continue the Sabbath school exuberance as we return home. Usually the children get out our set of felts and teach the Sabbath school lesson to us or to each other.

Then follows a scrumptious lunch, with some special delicacy that we do not have during the week.[7] The afternoons are times of adventure in the woods to learn secrets of nature and our God. (See the discussion in chapter 3.) Drawing upon many sources, we have joined others in gathering ideas for activities on Sabbath afternoon so that the Sabbath can be "made so interesting to our families that its weekly return will be hailed with joy."[8]

Our Sabbath evening worship has some features in common with the start of the Sabbath, but with a special spice—literally. Besides the candles and the singing and the praying, we pass around a spice box full of fresh aromas as a reminder of the sweet fragrance that we have just experienced in the Sabbath. Sometimes I read the "Havdalah" prayer chanted by our Sabbathkeeping Jewish brothers and sisters as they conclude the Sabbath:

> Blessed art Thou, Lord our God, King of the
> universe, who makes a division [havdalah]
> between the sacred and the secular,
> between light and darkness, between Israel and
> the other nations, between the seventh day and
> the six working days.
> Blessed art thou, Lord, who makes a distinction
> between the sacred and secular.[9]

Then we sing the Hebrew song "Eliahu HaNavi" ("Elijah the Prophet") and say to each other, "Shavua tov! (Happy new week!"). Instead of being eager to see the Sabbath end, our family is loathe to let it depart. We often prolong our worship long beyond the actual time of sunset. Each of us joins in little Jonathan's recurring tearful lament, "I wish Sabbath weren't over!"

Our family's way of celebrating the Sabbath is certainly not the required norm for everybody. God has planned the time—the seventh day from sunset to sunset—releasing us from the necessity of work on this day; but He allows us to plan the space, the activities, to make our fellowship with

A Song of Sanctification

Him meaningful. He has given us some general guidelines for optimum celebration through the example of Jesus and the counsel of Scripture and other inspired sources. But the specifics are ours, to create by careful thought and planning. Hear the word of the Lord, O singer of the Sabbath song: "Call the Sabbath an exquisite delight!"

Isaiah 58:13 couples the keynote of exquisite delight with two additional aspects of Sabbath observance that round out God's balanced counsel: We are to call the Sabbath not only (1) an exquisite delight, but also (2) the holy of the Lord, and (3) honorable. Let us look more closely at the second point, the Sabbath as God's holy day. This principle became especially meaningful in our household when we realized that *holy* means "set apart," or simply, "wholly for the Lord." [10]

Wholly for the Lord

For our family the Sabbath is "wholly for the Lord" in at least three ways. First, it is wholly for Him, *all of it,* even the edges of the Sabbath. The usual scene in our home used to be a mad rush on Friday afternoons. With harried minds and frayed nerves, we too often frantically cooked and cleaned until the last minute before sunset. Then we would flop down on the couch, exhausted but satisfied that we had started the Sabbath on time. We had—we thought—kept the fourth commandment to the letter.

When we became acquainted with some of the practices of our Jewish Sabbathkeeping friends, however, we took a long, hard look at the way we started the Sabbath. From the Jewish perspective, the Sabbath does not suddenly arrive at sunset Friday evenings. All Friday afternoon this royal queen is in the process of coming, and finally at set of sun she is completely here. Thus the aura of the holy hours spills over into the time of preparation, endowing it with special joy and peace. Long before the sun actually sets, the Jewish family has lit the candles and is ready and prepared in eager expectation for the full appearance of *Shabbat HaMalka*, Sabbath the queen.

A LOVE SONG FOR THE SABBATH

From the Christian perspective, does not the realization that the King of kings will soon be with us transform our Sabbath preparation from a mad rush to an eager expectancy? Can we not visualize Him casting His sanctifying influence over our final hours of preparation for His advent with the Sabbath? Yes, we will still clean the house, do the cooking, iron our clothes, polish our shoes, and take our baths[11]—all before the Sabbath begins. But not just in order to fulfill some legal requirements of a written code. The King is coming! Our Royal Lover will soon be here. We want to make our humble home as much like a palace and our persons as attractive as we can. Thus we do these things not just because we have to, but because when He arrives we don't want to miss a single moment of companionship with our beloved God. Yes, we "jealously guard the edges of the Sabbath"[12] because we are jealous lovers! Why would we want to be polishing shoes when we can be with the King, our friend? Work that we didn't get done we forget until the Sabbath is over.[13] On Sabbath we are free from the tyranny of toil, free for fellowship and celebration.

Proper preparation for the Sabbath takes careful planning. One does not meet the arrival of a king with hasty last-minute actions. Therefore we try to do some of the cooking and cleaning on Wednesday and Thursday, so Friday will not be such a hectic time. We consciously try to prepare not only our physical surroundings and bodies but also our souls. It makes sense that "before the Sabbath begins, the mind as well as the body should be withdrawn from worldly business."[14] By God's grace we prepare our hearts by putting away any differences that we have between us[15] and approach the Sabbath without hurrying, jostling, or impatience. We aim to start worship about a half hour before sundown, so that even if we are late, we're early.[16] This brings great composure to our family. It sets the tone of tranquility and peace that we want to maintain throughout the whole Sabbath day. When we fail to reach our ideal of beginning Sabbath early, we notice the difference!

A Song of Sanctification

A second aspect of Sabbath holiness to the Lord is that we are "wholly for Him," *all of us*, including our children.

This does not mean that we are restricting our children's enjoyment of the Sabbath; to the contrary, we recognize that "we are not to teach our children that they must not be happy on the Sabbath. . . . Parents, make the Sabbath a delight, that your children may look forward to it and have a welcome in their hearts for it." [17] Such an experience comes by "devising means to impart proper instruction and interesting them in spiritual things." [18] For parents willing to invest their time and interest in Sabbath holiness, for their children as well as themselves, the portion of holy time outside of the Sabbath worship services "may be made the most sacred and precious season of all the Sabbath hours." [19]

A third aspect of Sabbath holiness is that we are "wholly His," *all the time*, even when it isn't Sabbath. The same God who said "Remember the Sabbath day by keeping it holy" (Ex. 20:8) declared in almost the same breath, "You are to be my holy people" (Ex. 22:31), and again, "Be holy, because I am holy (Lev. 11:44, 45; see also 20:7; 1 Peter 1:15)." The Sabbath is a symbol of our entire life of sanctification, because "in order to keep the Sabbath holy, men must themselves be holy." [20] We cannot be wholly for ourselves during the week and wholly for the Lord on Sabbath. Those who are truly under the sign of the Sabbath will "understand its spiritual bearing upon all the transactions of life. . . . Daily it will be their prayer that the sanctification of the Sabbath may rest upon them. [21] Truly the Sabbath will become the day around which all other days of the week revolve, the embodiment of a holy life of companionship with Christ every day. While God offers His special presence on the Sabbath when we are free from secular cares, He is also available to walk with us in the midst of our secular occupations, turning even the most menial work into sacred moments spent in His presence.

A LOVE SONG FOR THE SABBATH

The Day of Honor

The Sabbath is not only an exquisite delight and holy to the Lord; it is "honorable." How does this principle clarify the meaning of Sabbath observance?

The Sabbath day is honorable because its observance brings honor to the Lord of the Sabbath. We call the day honorable by exalting the One to whom it points. As in any celebration, we bring honor to the esteemed guest by forgetting ourselves and focusing upon him or her. In Isaiah 58:13 God has given us three guidelines for honoring Him during the Sabbath day.

First, He can be exalted by "not doing your [own] ways." After a long week's hard work, the way of least resistance to many on the Sabbath, is to while away the day in "lay activities" in bed asleep. We can easily understand why Ellen White wrote:

> "It is displeasing to God for Sabbathkeepers to sleep during much of the Sabbath. They dishonor their Creator in so doing, and, by their example, say that the six days are too precious for them to spend in resting." [22]

I am one who often finds himself overtaken by a pleasant drowsiness after a good Sabbath meal, and I do not believe that it is always wrong to take a Sabbath afternoon nap. But it makes sense that if I sleep away the best hours of the Sabbath, what does it say about my love for the honored Guest who has come to spend time in fellowship with me? As much as possible, I want to savor every moment I can with my beloved King.

For some of us a bit more rested, there may come another temptation to "do our own ways." The word *ways* here literally means "roads," or "paths." It has a metaphorical sense, but perhaps there are some literal "paths" that will lead us to forget the honored Guest. Instead, we need to take those paths that will bring us to church, to places of nature, to someone's home to do good.

A Song of Sanctification

I fear that we often travel on this day when it might be avoided. . . . We should be more careful about traveling on the boats or cars on this day. . . . It may be necessary for us to travel on the Sabbath; but so far as possible we should secure our tickets and make all necessary arrangements on some other day. When starting on a journey we should make every possible effort to plan so as to avoid reaching our destination on the Sabbath.[23]

Again, this is not a legalistic regulation, but a beautiful principle. On the Lord's day of honor, I want to forget myself and focus upon Him. I want to eliminate every distraction that will divert my attention from my honored Guest who is also my beloved Friend. The Orthodox Jews refuse to engage in any kind of vehicular travel on the Sabbath. In Israel it is spectacular to see thousands of Jewish families walking to the synagogue every Sabbath, and though it is not a biblical rule, I think we would find far fewer heads nodding during the Sabbath sermon if a brisk walk to the church had stirred up the circulatory system.

Second, according to Isaiah 58:13, we can honor the Sabbath and exalt the Lord of the Sabbath by not "pursuing your own business" (margin, RSV), or by "not doing as you please" (NIV). As we have pointed out previously, it does not mean that the Sabbath should bring us no pleasure. In the immediate context, it probably refers most particularly to the pursuing of one's weekday business affairs. The scriptural injunction is clear: "Six days you shall labor, but on the seventh day you shall rest; even during the plowing season and harvest you must rest" (Ex. 34:21). Even in the busiest time of year God rescues us from the tyranny of toil. No secular business is so important as to rob us of fellowship with Him.

However, it does not mean that we should spend the Sabbath in inactivity. Interestingly, the word translated "made" in Exodus 31:17 ("the Lord *made* the heavens and the earth") is the same word translated "celebrate" in the

A LOVE SONG FOR THE SABBATH

preceding verse ("to *celebrate* the sabbath throughout their generations" [NASB]). As the NASB notes in the margin, to "celebrate" the Sabbath is literally to "do" the Sabbath. The Sabbath is a time for activity, for creative doing. But not our own business, our weekday affairs that cause us to take our minds off our beloved Sabbath Guest of honor.

The NIV translates the phrase in Isaiah 58:13 ("not seeking after your own business") as "not doing as you please." Here we encounter another nuance of the underlying rich Hebrew vocabulary. Once again God is not trying to make the Sabbath boring but rather to bring us to the highest joy. Doing "as you please" on the Sabbath is not good enough when the King comes visiting. As a boy, when Mother's Day arrived, I could have suggested we go mountain climbing together, then fix my bicycle and play a game of baseball. But somehow I don't think those activities would have brought either my mother or me the highest joy on her special day. The greatest delight came from doing those things together that honored her, that focused my personal attention upon her. Similarly, our highest joy on the Sabbath results as we engage in those activities that exalt God by centering our contemplation upon Him.

This simple principle helps us to determine what is appropriate recreation (or re-creation) on the Sabbath. We can ask, "Does this activity naturally lead me to think of God and His character, or does it tend to divert my attention from Him to the activity or to myself?" As our family has personally applied this concept, we have found that such outdoor activities as nature walks in the woods or along an isolated beach give us an opportunity to focus upon God's handiwork without distractions. We have a canoe docked at the river behind our house, and a Sabbath afternoon canoe ride affords us spectacular vistas of wildlife and opportunities to stop along the shore to collect fossils and shells. In the winter we "walk" through the fields on cross-country skis to observe the glories of winter beauty. Again the major emphasis is on God's works and not the activity or ourselves.

A Song of Sanctification

On the other hand we have found that such sports as waterskiing, ball games, sledding, and swimming—activities that our family enjoys—tend to center our attention upon what we are doing and do not seem to naturally lead our minds to think of God and His character. Certainly our decisions are not the norm for everyone, but I am convinced the principle of Isaiah 58:13 is sound. The Holy Spirit will lead each honest seeker to discover how he or she should apply the biblical principle in selecting appropriate Sabbath activities.

The third principle in our verse for honoring God is by not "speaking [idle or one's own] words." It is no doubt the most difficult for Sabbathkeepers to follow, and the one most often disregarded. We think of our conversation at the dinner table after Sabbath church services. How easily our own words can creep in: discussions of weekday activities and plans, business concerns, the latest fashions, or (heaven forbid!) the latest gossip. Quickly we recognize how difficult it is for the mind to be "disciplined to dwell upon sacred themes."[24] But through the help and strength of Christ it is possible to "conscientiously restrict" ourselves "to conversation upon religious themes—to present truth, present duty, the Christian's hopes and fears, trials, conflicts, and afflictions; to overcoming at last, and the reward to be received."[25]

Again we do this not because we *have to,* but because we *love to;* not in order to obey a command, but because we're in love with the Divine Royal Guest and want to talk of our love. To those deeply in love, common ordinary conversation about everyday affairs pales into insignificance as they speak of their feelings for each other. Let us then treasure in our hearts the thought that our beloved God sanctifies the Sabbath through His own divine presence. If we cultivate a sense of His loving presence on the Sabbath, conversing about that love will become more and more spontaneous. As long as we do not short-circuit the fellowship by our own ways or business or words, we cannot help being sanctified—falling more deeply in divine love!

A LOVE SONG FOR THE SABBATH

We cannot leave our discussion of Sabbath observance in light of Isaiah 58 without noticing one more fact that has recently come to my attention. Several commentators rightly point out that the first and last parts of Isaiah 58 are intricately united.[26]

As we have already noted, the context of the chapter is that of the Day of Atonement, and therefore the entire chapter is a revelation of true Sabbath observance during the antitypical day of atonement. The early verses of Isaiah 58 direct us not to a fast from food but to the nature of the true *fast* on our Day of Atonement Sabbaths:

> Is not this the kind of fasting I have chosen: to loose the chains of injustice and untie the cords of the yoke, to set the oppressed free and break every yoke? Is it not to share your food with the hungry and to provide the poor wanderer with shelter—when you see the naked, to clothe him, and not to turn away from your own flesh and blood? (Isa. 8:6, 7).

Here Isaiah emphasizes the humanitarian, redemptive function of the Sabbath that Jesus stressed later in His Sabbath healing miracles. As Jesus reminded us; "My Father is always at his work to this very day, and I, too, am working" (John 5:17). "Therefore it is lawful to do good on the Sabbath" (Matt. 12:11).

A colleague of mine at Andrews University recently underscored for me the crucial importance of such activity on the Sabbath. He helped me balance my emphasis upon a Sabbath of *celebration* with a complimentary vista into a Sabbath of *service*. As a result, I have been pondering how we can more effectively implement this principle in our family.

A Day of Service

Perhaps we have already been on the right track as we have occasionally invited home for Sabbath dinner local church members who have no family and few friends, and

A Song of Sanctification

as we have opened our home for times of fellowship with students far from home.

It is a start, but I am becoming more convinced that the divinely ordained "Sabbath fast" goes beyond the confines of our own church. There is the jail in nearby Benton Harbor, the rest home and hospital just a short distance away from my house. A number of lonely shut-ins live not too far away. Jail bands and singing bands organized by the church may be the answer for some. If they are not organized so that my whole family can participate together, perhaps we can form our own little singing band and go to the nearby rest home. We recently explored the possibility of forming lasting friendships with developmentally-retarded individuals in the community, and the local social service agency has been eager to cooperate.

Recently a pastor friend of mine related a story that opened up whole new possibilities for experiencing a Sabbath of service. Isaiah 58:10 calls upon us to "satisfy the needs of the oppressed." In a district in the South the local Seventh-day Adventist church had few members and little influence in the community. The pastor held an evangelistic series, and not a single nonmember showed up.

But about that time a newly converted Adventist plumber moved into the community. The man didn't have the necessary qualifications to give Bible studies or participate in singing bands—but he was an excellent plumber. So every Sabbath afternoon he loaded his tools in the back of his pickup truck and set off down the road. He stopped at every place where it looked like someone "oppressed" might be living—the poor, the widows, the disabled, etc. Then he simply inquired if they had any plumbing that needed fixing. After he completed the job and the individual he had helped asked how much he wanted, the plumber replied, "No charge! This is God's gift to you on His holy Sabbath." Sabbath after Sabbath—throughout the town—"God's gift to you on His holy Sabbath."

The next year another evangelistic meeting took place in the local church, and the church had standing room only. It seemed as if almost the whole town had shown up, eager to learn about the plumber's God and His Sabbath.

As I listened to the first part of this story, I must admit that thoughts ran through my mind such as *that man is working on the Sabbath.* Hospital work to relieve suffering is OK, but plumbing on Sabbath?" However, by the end I wondered whether perhaps the plumber had captured the essence of Isaiah's call to "satisfy the needs of the oppressed" and of Jesus' statement "My Father is always at his work . . . and I, too, am working." My pastor friend concluded the story with a challenge: "What would happen if a whole group of teenagers went down the road on Sabbath afternoon armed with hoes and rakes and shovels and paintbrushes and paint, not to earn money, but with the phrase 'God's gift for you on the Sabbath'?"

I confess that the thought still jars my traditional understanding of Sabbath observance as refraining from all unnecessary work. Perhaps such humanitarian excursions into the community could come on another day besides Sabbath. But maybe my understanding of the serving function of Sabbath needs to grow! Thus I'm still pondering the concept in my heart.

Whether or not we agree with the appropriateness of the plumber's Sabbath activities, I trust the story has expanded our horizons to think of creative ways to serve our fellowmen in the spirit of the Isaiah 58 Sabbath fast—as God's gift to them on His Sabbath.

The Promised Blessing

For those who enter into the celebration and service of the Sabbath as described in Isaiah 58, a glorious blessing awaits them: "Then you will find your joy in the Lord, and I will cause you to ride on the heights of the land and to feast on the inheritance of your father Jacob. The mouth of the Lord has spoken" (Isa. 58:14).

A Song of Sanctification

Have you experienced the blessings of Sabbath-keeping? Has the Sabbath become a weekly sign of your ongoing sanctification? May I encourage you in the words of John Wesley:

> The Lord not only hallowed the Sabbath-day, but He hath also blessed it. So that you are an enemy to yourself. You throw away your own blessing if you neglect to keep this day holy. It is a day of special grace. The King of heaven now sits upon His mercy seat in a more gracious manner than on other days, to bestow blessings on those that observe it. If you love your own soul, can you forbear laying hold on so happy an opportunity? Awake, arise, let God give thee His blessing! Receive a token of His love; cry to Him that thou mayest sing the riches of His grace and mercy in Christ Jesus![27]

Fellow singer of the ninety-second psalm, let us proclaim joyfully the sanctification of the Sabbath!

> Thou, Lord, has high exalted me
> With royal strength and dignity;
> With throne anointing I am blest,
> Thy grace and favor on me rest;
> I thus exult o'er all my foes,
> O'er all that would escape oppose (Ps. 92:10-12, paraphrased).

References

[1] White, *The Desire of Ages*, p. 288.

[2] _____, *Testimonies,* vol. 6, p. 351.

[3] Sakae Kubo, *God Meets Man: A Theology of the Sabbath and Second Advent* (Nashville: Southern Pub. Assn., 1978), p. 52.

[4] See John F. A. Sawyer, *Isaiah* (Philadelphia: Westminster, 1986), vol. 2, pp. 172-174, for further discussion. Note in particular the call of the shophar, or ram's horn, in Isaiah 58:1 (cf. Lev. 25:9); the reference to fasting and humbling of oneself in verses 3 and 5 (literally, "afflicting of souls," the same words as in Lev. 23:27-32); and the mention of the "acceptable day of the Lord" (verse 5), alluding to Isaiah 61:2, language of the jubilee that commenced on the Day of Atonement.

A LOVE SONG FOR THE SABBATH

[5] See White, *The Great Controversy*, pp. 409-432, 479-491, for further discussion.

[6] See _____*Testimonies*, vol. 6, p. 355: "Many need instruction as to how they should appear in the assembly for worship on the Sabbath. They are not to enter the presence of God in the common clothing worn during the week. All should have a special Sabbath suit, to be worn when attending service in God's house."

[7] "Let the meals, though simple, be palatable and attractive. Provide something that will be regarded as a treat, something the family do not have every day." (*Ibid.*, p. 357).

[8] *Ibid.*, vol. 2, p. 585.

[9] See Millgram, *Sabbath: The Day of Delight*, pp. 88-91, for the complete *Havdalah* service.

[10] See White, *Desire of Ages*, p. 556; White, *Christ's Object Lessons*, p. 48; *The SDA Bible Commentary*, Ellen White Comments, vol. 7, p. 1076; cf. the scholarly discussion along similar lines summarized in Nilton Amorim, "Desecration and Defilement in the Old Testament." (Ph.D. diss., Andrews University, 1985), pp. 147-162.

[11] See Ex. 16:15-30. The sixth day (Friday) is called the preparation day in Mark 15:42. Compare White, *Testimonies*, vol. 6, p. 355: "On Friday let the preparation for the Sabbath be completed. See that all the clothing is in readiness and that all the cooking is done. Let the boots be blacked and the baths be taken. It is possible to do this. If you make it a rule, you can do it."

[12] White, *Testimonies*, vol. 6, p. 356.

[13] _____, *Patriarchs and Prophets* (Mountain View, Calif.: Pacific Press Pub. Assn., 1958), p. 296: "Work that is neglected until the beginning of the Sabbath should remain undone until it is past."

[14] _____, *Testimonies*, vol. 6, p. 356.

[15] _____ "There is another work that should receive attention on the preparation day. On this day all differences between brethren, whether in the family or in the church, should be put away. Let all bitterness and wrath and malice be expelled from the soul" (*Ibid.*).

[16] "Before the setting of the sun let the members of the family assemble to read God's Word, to sing and pray" (*Ibid.*).

[17] _____, *Child Guidance* (Washington, D.C.: Review and Herald Pub. Assn., 1982), pp. 533-536.

[18] _____, *Testimonies*, vol. 2, p. 582.

[19] *Ibid.*, vol. 6, p. 357.

[20] _____, *The Desire of Ages*, p. 283.

[21] _____, *Testimonies*, vol. 6, p. 353.

[22] *Ibid.*, vol. 2, p. 704.

[23] *Ibid.*, vol. 6, pp. 359, 360.

[24] *Ibid.*, vol. 2, p. 703.

[25] *Ibid.*, p. 704.

[26] See, e.g., James Muilenberg, "The Book of Isaiah: Chapters 40-66," in G. A. Buttrick, ed., *The Interpreter's Bible* (New York, Nashville: Abingdon Press, 1956), vol. 5, p. 677.

[27] John Wesley, "A Word to a Sabbath Breaker: 'Remember the Sabbath-day to keep it holy,' " *Admonitions to Persons of Various Descriptions*, Tract VI.

Chapter 6

A Song of Glorification

[Trans-planted] in the house of the Lord,
they will flourish in the courts of our God.
They will still bear fruit in old age,
they will [ever] stay fresh and green,
proclaiming, "The Lord is upright; he is my Rock,
and there is no wickedness in him.
—Ps. 92:13-15

As we sing the Sabbath song of sanctification described in the preceding chapter, we will experience a foretaste of heaven, the message proclaimed in the final stanza of Psalm 92. Verse 13 literally reads, *"Transplanted* into the house of the Lord, they will flourish in the courts of our God." Here the Hebrew word for *transplanted* is a technical term referring to the eschatological (last-day) entrance into the future life in the heavenly courts of God.[1] Continuing the imagery of palm and cedar, God promises that because of our "heavenly transplant" (the resurrection or translation) we will still bring forth fruit in old age. In fact, we will be "ever full of sap and green" (verse 14, RSV). According to this stanza, the Sabbath is a celebration in anticipation of glorification.

From Eden to Eden

Even before the Fall, the seventh-day Sabbath hinted of the eschatological rest. So writes Geerhardus Vos:

A LOVE SONG FOR THE SABBATH

The Sabbath brings the principle of the eschatological structure of history to bear upon the mind of man after a symbolical and typical fashion. It teaches its lesson through the rhythmical succession of six days of labor and one ensuing day of rest in each successive week. Man is reminded in this way that life is not an aimless existence, that a goal lies beyond. This was true before, and apart from, redemption. The eschatological is an older strand in revelation than the soteric.[2]

The Sabbath links us in unbroken succession from Eden in the beginning to Eden restored. We have seen repeatedly throughout this book how the Sabbath is an experience of the presence of God. God makes the day holy by gracing it with His presence, and He makes the worshipers holy who enter into that precious Sabbath fellowship. In the Garden of Eden, Adam and Eve had the privilege of participating in face-to-face communion with their Maker. But as we have seen, sin interrupted that open communication between man and God. The Sabbath remained, nonetheless, as the vital link of divine-human fellowship. By faith man met his appointment with God on the seventh day and basked in the loving presence of his intimate Friend.

In a special way, that Friend embodied the meaning of Sabbath rest. He became Immanuel—"God with us." The incarnate Christ made it possible once more for man to enjoy open communion with God. His coming brought about the spiritual inauguration of the Sabbath-rest epitomized by the Sabbath (see Heb. 4). By faith in Him, true Christians of all generations already have come "to Mount Zion, to the heavenly Jerusalem, the city of the living God"; "to thousands upon thousands of angels in joyful assembly"; and ultimately, "to Jesus, the mediator of a new covenant" (Heb. 12:22-24).

And yet a future "promise of entering his rest still stands" (Heb. 4:1). As the new Joshua, Jesus wants to lead His redeemed people *literally* into the heavenly Promised

A Song of Glorification

Land. The ultimate fulfillment of what the Sabbath epitomizes will come when "the dwelling of God is with men, and he will live with them. They will be his people, and God himself will be with them and be their God. He will wipe every tear from their eyes. There will be no more death or mourning or crying or pain, for the old order of things has passed away" (Rev. 21:3-4).

Eden will be restored! God will remove the curses of sin—death and mourning and crying and pain; thorns and thistles and work by the sweat of man's brow; hostility between man and beast; physical deformities and mental deficiencies. Best of all, the barrier to face-to-face fellowship with God will vanish forever.

Once more humanity will enjoy the Sabbath in its original function of open communion between man and his Creator. Thus in the setting of the restoration of God's rule (see Isa. 66:22), we find a description of the eternal continuation of the weekly Sabbath: "'From one New Moon to another and from one Sabbath to another, all mankind will come and bow down before me,' says the Lord" (verse 23). In Eden made new the Sabbath is no longer a test of loyalty, even as it was not in the beginning in Eden. Instead, all the redeemed will come and worship on it as God's day of extraspecial communion with them. They will find it their greatest joy and most natural wish to be in the presence of their beloved Lord from Sabbath to Sabbath.

What Sabbaths those will be with God in eternity! First, they will be celebrations of *Creation* (and the new creation), with the Creator Himself opening before us the marvels of the universe and the lessons they teach about His character. Second, they will be grand celebrations of *redemption*—eternal, full, and free—with the Redeemer Himself unfolding the mysteries of the conflict between good and evil and the deeper wonders of His redeeming love. Third, they will be celebrations of *sanctification*, with the Holy Sanctifier Himself to lead us to ever loftier heights of holiness infused by His intimate presence. And fourth, they will be celebrations of *glorification*, with the Glorifier Himself unfolding new glories to admire and experience. And all of these revelations coalesce in mightier and still mightier motivations to joyous praise. Can you imagine the unspeakable thrill as "ten thousand times ten thousand and thousands of thousands of voices unite to swell the mighty chorus of praise?"[3]

A Foretaste of Heaven

When you think of Sabbaths in the new earth spent with God, the angels, and our fellow redeemed saints, do you, like me, yearn for that day? Do you long to experience that heavenly bliss *now*?

Seems I cannot wait; yearning to enter Zion's pearly gate.

Well, the good news of the Sabbath is that heavenly bliss can be ours in the here and now! The Sabbath is a foretaste of heaven. The Jews of old caught the vision of the Sabbath as "the anticipation, the foretaste, the paradigm, of life in the world to come."[4] A Midrashic allegory dramatizes their understanding:

Israel said before the Holy One, blessed be He: "Master of the world, if we observe the commandments, what reward will we have?" He said to them: "The world to come." They said to Him: "Show us its likeness." He showed them the Sabbath.

John Calvin grasped this insight for Protestantism when he wrote: "The Lord through the seventh-day has sketched for His people the coming perfection of His Sabbath in the last day."[5]

Long before Calvin or the Jewish allegory, Isaiah described the exquisite delight (*oneg*) and glory (*kābod*) of the Sabbath (see Isaiah 58:13) as an echo of the same exquisite delight (*oneg*) and glory (*kābod*) of the end of days (Isa. 66:11).[6] From the prophet's use of this key Hebrew word,

A Song of Glorification

"the implication is clear. The delight and joy that will mark the end of days is made available here and now by the Sabbath."[7]

The author of Hebrews recognized that the future promise of rest in the heavenly Canaan (see Heb. 4:1), epitomized in the Sabbath (see verse 9), is already available to the Christian.

And the psalmist heard the music of the heavenly Sabbath, for the themes that will lift us up on wings of song in the new earth—Creation, redemption, sanctification, and glorification—he embodied in his song for the Sabbath (Ps. 92). What we will celebrate for eternity we can already begin to share in now through the Sabbath. What will thrill our souls then can even now give us exquisite delight.

So, fellow singers of the Sabbath song, we may conduct ourselves on Sabbath as if the future age has already come! On Sabbath we get a foretaste of that eternal calm and freedom from the pressures of life. We can feel ourselves liberated from the tyranny of time and schedules and work responsibilities that weigh us down. On the Sabbath we bask in that heavenly atmosphere unpolluted by cruel competition. Each seventh day we savor that bliss of eternal joy and exquisite delight. All week long we face a humdrum existence, often without adequate satisfaction and delight, but on Sabbath we taste pure joy.

In our Sabbath services, "to those who worship God in spirit and in truth and in the beauty of holiness it will be as the gate of heaven."[8] At home, "on this day [Sabbath] more than on any other, it is possible for us to live the life of Eden."[9] Released by God from the demands of toil, our families, like Adam and Eve in Eden, may have blessed "opportunity for communion with Him, with nature, and with one another."[10]

Every 24-hour seventh day is an oasis of time in which we can have a foretaste of that intimate fellowship in the heavenly house of God. Every Sabbath God invites us, as it were, to come to His celestial palace to have a glimpse of heaven. During its holy hours we savor the heavenly life that will in eternity have no end. As the Psalmist has written, even in "old age we will still be young, full of that green verdure of the palm and the cedar" (Ps. 92:14, paraphrased).

Sabbath Hope

Because the Sabbath anticipates heaven, it gives meaning and purpose to our lives on earth. On Sabbath we see most clearly our transcendent goal of everlasting joy, quickening us to a heavenly hope. The Sabbath is a guarantee of eternity. In the bustle and jostle of the workplace it keeps us from losing sight of our heavenly goal. It enables us to work now with an eye to eternity. Facing an age of secular materialism, the Sabbath assures us that there is a future life worth everything it may take to reach it. Through the Sabbath we know that all the fortune and fame, all the power and prestige, and all the possessions on our planet, are "meaningless, a chasing after of the wind," (Eccl. 1:14), without the heavenly hope.

As we joyfully anticipate the approach of the Sabbath each week, we assume the posture of one eagerly anticipating the age to come. And as the Sabbath comes at the end of the week, "each weekly cycle reinforces our sense of movement toward the future. If the weekdays constitute a journey toward Sabbath rest and peace, it enhances our certainty that all of life represents a journey toward rest and peace."[11] Thus we have no fear of the future, for what the Sabbath is like, with all of its joys and delights, we know the world made new will also be like—and much more. The blessed Sabbath hope "is like a precious stone, a thing to delight in and to grasp hold of in sheer wonderment and gratitude." It is "a prism, a multifaceted jewel, refracting throughout our lives the fullness of God's glory."[12] Even more, it is, yes, a song of love, a symphony of joy, an oratorio of exquisite delight.

The Glorification of God

How does the song of love for the Sabbath end? How do we sum up the meaning of the Sabbath? The last verse of

A Song of Glorification

the ninety-second psalm reiterates the underlying theme that has resurfaced again and again. It is all toward one end: "To show that the Lord is upright; he is my rock, and there is no unrighteousness in him" (verse 15, RSV). The focal point of the psalm, of the Sabbath, is a revelation of the character of God. The psalm began: "It is good to praise the Lord and make music to your name [character], O Most High, to proclaim your love in the morning and your faithfulness at night." The center point came in verse 8: "But you, O Lord, are exalted forever." And now the conclusion takes up the same refrain.

As we have seen earlier, we are caught up in a cosmic conflict where the adversary has claimed that God is not as the psalmist describes Him, that He is arbitrary, unjust, unfair, and unworthy of our allegiance. The psalm for the Sabbath proclaims that Satan is wrong. God is our all-powerful and all-loving *Creator*, our glorious *Redeemer*, both in the past and in the future. The Lord is our intimate *Sanctifier*, making us grow ever more like Him. And He is our magnificent *Glorifier*, even now giving each one of us a foretaste of His glory. Man, what a God!

In short, the message of this psalm, of the Sabbath, is not ultimately about *our* glorification, which we eagerly await. Rather, it is, in the final analysis, about the glorification of *God*. The message of the Sabbath is—"To God be the glory!"

I invite you to let the message of God's glory in the Sabbath so saturate your being, so fill your vision, that God, your Creator, Redeemer, Sanctifier, and Glorifier, may fill you to overflowing with eternal praise and joy—indeed, exquisite delight.

The righteous man shall flourish well,
And in the house of God shall dwell;
He shall be like a goodly tree,
And all his life shall fruitful be;
For righteous is the Lord and just,

A LOVE SONG FOR THE SABBATH

He is my rock, in Him I trust
(Ps. 92:13-15, paraphrased).

References

[1] See Mitchel Dahood, *Psalms II: 51-100*, in _____, ed., *The Anchor Bible* (Garden City, N.Y.: Doubleday and Co., 1968), p. 338; cf. vol. 1, pp. 3-4; Julia Morgenstern, *Hebrew Union College Annual* 16 (1941) : 81, 222.

[2] Geerhardus Vos, *Notes on Biblical Theology* (Grand Rapids: William B. Eerdmans, 1971), p. 156-157, cited in G. N. Davies, "The Christian Sabbath," *Reformed Theological Review* 42 (1983): 34.

[3] White, *The Great Controversy*, p. 678.

[4] Theodore Friedman, "The Sabbath: Anticipation of Redemption," *Judaism* 16 (1967): 443.

[5] John Calvin, *Institutes of the Christian Religion* (Philadelphia: Westminster, 1950), p. 396; ed., Roy Branson, in *Festival of the Sabbath*, p. 77.

[6] See the discussion in Friedman, p. 445.

[7] *Ibid.*

[8] White, *Testimonies*, vol. 6, p. 363.

[9] _____, *Education*, p. 250.

[10] *Ibid.*, p. 251.

[11] Scriven, *Jubilee of the World*, p. 30.

[12] Branson, p. 78.

Chapter 7

A Psalm of Life

As a college student I once had to memorize a poem by Henry Wadsworth Longfellow. Entitled "A Psalm of Life," it made a deep impact upon my mind. Perhaps you recall some of those famous words:

> Lives of great men all remind us
> We can make our lives sublime,
> And, departing, leave behind us
> Footprints on the sands of time.
>
> Footprints, that perhaps another,
> Sailing o'er life's solemn main,
> A forlorn and shipwrecked brother,
> Seeing, shall take heart again.
>
> Let us, then, be up and doing,
> With a heart for any fate;
> Still achieving, still pursuing,
> Learn to labor and to wait.

It was actually the second stanza—part of which is not theologically correct—that provided my watchword during those college years:

> Life is real! Life is earnest!
> And the grave is not its goal;
> Dust thou art, to dust returnest,
> Was not spoken of the soul.

A LOVE SONG FOR THE SABBATH

Never mind that Longfellow was wrong and that the soul does die—until the resurrection (see Gen. 2:7; Eze. 18:4)—I was interested in that phrase "Life is real!" I remember driving my new 1967 Volkswagen Beetle with my fiancée and another couple through a snowstorm in the Colorado Rockies. As a native southern Californian, it was my first experience navigating in snow, and when suddenly the Volkswagon skidded out of control, I jammed the brakes instead of downshifting, and we slid into the side of a mountain. Jumping out of the car, I looked at the damage and, in a rare moment of self-control, exclaimed, "Life is real!"

I wish I could say that Longfellow's "Psalm of Life" has always stood me in as good stead as then. Actually, as profound as his poem may be, another "psalm of life" has captured my attention and admiration eclipsing Longfellow's creation in my mind. It is the ninety-second psalm, the psalm for the Sabbath, which we have been studying throughout this book.

Personal study of the Sabbath in Scripture has convinced me that its intrinsic nature as holy, consecrated time embraces the essence of the consecrated life that God designs should be ours. If such be the case, then it follows that the one psalm for the Sabbath in Scripture is nothing less than the ultimate psalm of life. From studying Psalm 92 in recent months, I have come to the conviction that its message indeed captures the significance not only of the Sabbath but of the consecrated life. It has become for me and my household—and I invite you to adopt it for yourselves—a psalm of life.

That the Sabbath embodies the essence of the Christian life is not original with me. The author of Hebrews has clearly shown that the weekly Sabbath rest epitomizes the rest of grace that we may continually find in Christ (see Heb. 4). Matthew juxtaposes Christ's Sabbath activities with His great invitation: "Come to me, all you who are weary and burdened, and I will give you rest" (Matt. 11:28; cf. Matt. 12:1-14). Ellen White confirmed that "the divine influence resting upon the Sabbath may attend [us] through

A Psalm of Life

the week."[1] She encourages Christians to understand the Sabbath's "spiritual bearing upon all the transactions of life" and to pray daily "that the sanctification of the Sabbath may rest upon them."[2]

Abraham Heschel has beautifully described how the Sabbath is the focal point for our whole lives:

> All days of the week must be spiritually consistent with the day of days. All our life should be a pilgrimage to the seventh day; the thought and appreciation of what this day may bring to us should be ever-present in our minds. For the Sabbath is the counterpoint of living; the melody sustained throughout all agitations and vicissitudes which menace our conscience; our awareness of God's presence in the world. What we are depends on what the Sabbath is to us.[3]

Again Heschel writes: "The Sabbath is the inspirer; the other days the inspired."[4] In other words, "When we truly keep the Sabbath, the days become opportunities to *embody* what the Sabbath stands for, to give strong bones and warm flesh to mere words."[5]

One more expression of this same beautiful thought:

> That which is set apart from other things as "holy" is so distinguished only in order that it may imbue with holiness and consecration also every phase of life taking place beyond its confines. Light is set apart from darkness only so that it may give life and growth to the forces and materials that have gathered in the darkness. . . . In the same manner, the seventh day was set apart from the six working days only so that its Sabbath spirit might permeate all of weekday life.[6]

Our family has found the sentiments expressed by others to be true in our own experience. As we joyously celebrate the Sabbath, the atmosphere of rest and peace seems to spill over into the coming week. The Divine Guest

A LOVE SONG FOR THE SABBATH

who comes on Sabbath casts the aura of His presence over every other day.

Not only does the experience of the Sabbath influence all of our life, but its meaning structures our whole existence. I rejoice as I think how the Sabbath really provides the answer to the three most basic questions in life: Where do we come from? Why are we here? and Where do we go after we die? The three great quests of the philosophers through the ages—Whence? Why? Whither?—receive three profound answers in the Sabbath.

Whence? The Sabbath perpetually reminds us that "in the beginning God created the heavens and the earth." Why? The Sabbath points us to the divine plan of redemption and sanctification to restore man to the image of God. Whither? The Sabbath is the assurance, even the foretaste, of the final glorification in the world to come.

And overreaching all these questions and answers, the Sabbath points us to the ultimate source of all meaning— God Himself. In its holy hours we find God the Creator, Redeemer, Sanctifier, and Glorifier. And He is none other than Immanuel, God with us—Jesus Christ. In the Sabbath we meet Jesus. Fellowship with Him—what else matters? We find that He is the kind of God whom the Sabbath proclaims Him to be. Beholding such a God, we come to love Him ever more deeply, and break forth into ever more exuberant songs of praise.

Ultimately we discover that the real essence of life is that of praising God. Like the ancient Hebrew, we come to know that the praise of God is the primary reason for existence. God "is enthroned on the praises of Israel" (Ps. 22:3, paraphrased). Where there is real life, there is praise of Yahweh. Instead of Shakespeare's axiom "To be or not to be, that is the question," we find the scriptural axiom "To praise Him or not to praise Him, that is the question."

An experience with the God of the Sabbath transforms the melody of our life into one of celebration and praise. The song for the Sabbath becomes our great anthem of praise. We join our fellow Sabbathkeepers in singing the

A Psalm of Life

Sabbath love song, the psalm of life. The chorus swells until we realize that we are part of a multitude of singers, a cosmic choir comprised of all intelligent beings in the universe. Then all of creation, animate and inanimate, raises its unnumbered voices in unparalleled crescendo.

According to an old Jewish allegory, even the personified Sabbath joins in:

> Thereupon the Sabbath rose from its seat, and prostrated herself before God, saying: It is a good thing *to give thanks unto the Lord*. And the whole of creation added: And to sing praise unto Thy name, O Most High.[7]

Fellow singers of the Sabbath song, the size of the Sabbath chorus may seem small now, as seen by human eyes. But regardless of appearances, on the authority of Scripture and in love for the Holy Lamb, come, let our voices continue to burst forth with the song for the Sabbath. Sing it as a real song on the Sabbath (see the Appendix for arrangements). Sing it as a song of experience—on the Sabbath and as our daily psalm of life. Sing it to our friends and those who have never heard and been enthralled by its strains. Sing it in continual praise—"To God be the glory." And, praise God, soon the day of glorification will come, and we will join with "every creature in heaven and on earth and under the earth and on the sea" (Rev. 5:13) in the majestic refrain: "You, O Lord, are exalted forever!"

References

[1] White, *Testimonies*, vol. 2, p. 704.

[2] *Ibid.*, vol. 6, p. 353.

[3] Heschel, *The Sabbath*, p. 89.

[4] *Ibid.*, p. 22.

[5] Scriven, *Jubilee of the World*, p. 22.

[6] *Hirsch Siddur*, p. 567, cited in Richard Siegel, Michael Strassfeld, and Sharon Strassfeld, eds., *The First Jewish Catalog*, (Philadelphia: Jewish Publication Society of America), p. 113.

[7] Heschel, p. 24.

How Good It Is to Thank the Lord

Psalm 92

MELITA 8.8.8.8.8.8.
John B. Dykes

1. How good it is to thank the Lord, And praise to Thee, Most High ac-cord, To show Thy love with morn-ing light, And tell Thy faith-ful-ness each night; Yea, good it is Thy praise to sing, And all our sweet-est mu-sic bring.

2. O Lord, with joy my heart ex-pands Be-fore the won-ders of Thy hands; Great works, Je-ho-vah, Thou hast wrought, Ex-ceed-ing deep Thine ev-ery thought; A fool-ish man knows not their worth, Nor he whose mind is of the earth.

3. When as the grass the wick-ed grow when sin-ners flour-ish here be-low, Then is there end-less ru-in nigh, But Thou, O Lord, art throned on high; Thy foes shall fall be-fore Thy might, The wick-ed shall be put to flight.

4. Thou, Lord, hast high ex-alt-ed me with roy-al strength and dig-ni-ty; With Thine a-noint-ing I am blest, Thy grace and fa-vor on me rest; I thus ex-alt o'er all my foes, O'er all that would my cause op-pose.

5. The righ-teous man shall flour-ish well, And in the house of God shall dwell; He shall be like a good-ly tree, And all his life shall fruit-ful be; For righ-teous is the Lord and just, He is my rock, in Him I trust.

How Good It Is to Thank the Lord

Psalm 92

CHRISTINE L.M.
Ernest R. Kroeger

1. How good it is to thank the Lord, And praise to
2. O Lord, with joy my heart ex-pands Be-fore the
3. When as the grass the wick-ed grow, When sin-ners
4. Thou, Lord, hast high ex-alt-ed me With roy-al
5. The righ-teous man shall flour-ish well, And in the

Thee, Most High, ac-cord, To show Thy love with morn-ing light,
won-ders of Thy hands; Great works, Je-hov-ah Thou hast wrought
flour-ish here be-low, Then is there end-less ru-in nigh,
strength and dig-ni-ty; With Thine a-noint-ing I am blest,
house of God shall dwell; He shall be like a good-ly tree,

And tell Thy faith-ful-ness each night; Yea, good it
Ex-ceed-ing deep Thine ev-ery thought; A fool-ish
But Thou, O Lord, art throned on high; Thy foes shall
Thy grace and fa-vor on me rest; I thus ex-
And all his life shall fruit-ful be; For righ-teous

is Thy praise to sing, And all our sweet-est mu-sic bring.
man knows not their worth, Nor he whose mind is of the earth.
fall be-fore Thy might, The wick-ed shall be put to flight.
ult o'er all my foes, O'er all that would my cause op-pose.
is the Lord and just, He is my rock, in Him I trust.

Sabbath Eve

Psalm 92
Florence Weisberg

Henry Gideon

1. How good it is to thank the Lord,
2. With joy - ous psalms and with the harp,
3. Like state - ly palm the righ - teous thrive,
4. Still, in old age, ripe fruit they bear,

To praise Thy name, O Thou Most High;
Will I Thy mar - vels glad - ly sing;
As ce - dar fair they flour - ish free
Ver - dant and fresh they still re - main

To tell Thy kind - ness through the day, Thy
Thy works have made my heart re - joice; I
In God's own house; His courts a - lone Their
To prove that God, my Rock of Help, His

faith - ful - ness when night draws nigh.
tri - umph in Thy work, my King!
dwell - ing - place and home shall be.
righ - teous - ness doth e'er main - tain.

Sabbath Eve

Psalm 92
Florence Weisberg

From Lewandowski's *L'cho Dodee*

1. How good it is to thank the Lord,
2. With joy - ous psalms and with the harp,
3. Like state - ly palm the righ - teous thrive,
4. Still, in old age, ripe fruit they bear,

To praise Thy name, O Thou Most High;
Will I Thy mar - vels glad - ly sing;
As ce - dar fair they flour - ish free
Ver - dant and fresh they still re - main

To tell Thy kind - ness through the day,
Thy works have made my heart re - joice;
In God's own house; His courts a - lone
To prove that God, my Rock of Help,

Thy faith - ful - ness when night draws nigh.
I tri - umph in Thy work, my King!
Their dwell - ing - place and home shall be.
His righ - teous - ness doth e'er main - tain.

It Is Good to Sing Thy Praises

Psalm 92

ELLENDIE 8.7.8.7.D.
In Joshua Leavitt's *Christian Lyre.* 1831

1. It is good to sing Thy prais - es And to thank Thee,
2. Thou hast filled my heart with glad - ness Thro' the works Thy
3. But the good shall live be - fore Thee, Plant - ed in Thy

O Most High, Show - ing forth Thy lov - ing kind - ness
hands have wrought; Thou hast made my life vic - to - rious,
dwell - ing - place, Fruit - ful trees and ev - er ver - dant,

When the morn - ing lights the sky. It is good when
Great Thy works and deep Thy thought. Thou, O Lord, on
Nour - ished by Thy bound - less grace. In His good - ness

night is fall - ing Of Thy faith - ful - ness to tell, While with
high ex - alt - ed, Reign - est ev - er - more in might; All Thine
to the righ - teous God His righ - teous·ness dis- plays; God my

sweet, me - lo - dious prais- es Songs of ad - o - ra - tion swell.
en - e - mies shall per - ish, Sin be ban - ished from Thy sight.
rock, my strength and ref - uge, Just and true are all His ways.

Sweet Is the Work

Psalm 92
Isaac Watts

ST. POLYCARP. L.M.
I. J. Pleyel

1. Sweet is the work, my God, my King, To praise Thy name, give thanks and sing; To show Thy love by morning light, And talk of all Thy truth at night.

2. Sweet is the day of sacred rest, No mortal cares can seize my breast; Oh, may my heart in tune be found, Like David's harp of solemn sound.

3. My heart shall triumph in the Lord, And bless His works, and bless His Word; Thy works of grace, how bright they shine, How deep Thy counsels, how Divine!

4. Lord, I shall share a glorious part When grace hath well refined my heart, And fresh supplies of joy are shed, Like holy oil, to cheer my head.

A - men.

5. Sin, my worst enemy before,
Shall vex my eyes and ears no more;
My inward foes shall all be slain,
Nor Satan break my peace again.

6. Then shall I see, and hear, and know
All I desired or wished below,
And every power find sweet employ
In that eternal world of joy.